Joseph Addison Alexander

Joseph Addison Alexander of Princeton

Allan M. Harman

EP BOOKS
Faverdale North
Darlington
DL3 0PH, England

www.epbooks.org
sales@epbooks.org

EP BOOKS are distributed in the USA by:
JPL Fulfillment
3741 Linden Avenue Southeast,
Grand Rapids, MI 49548.

E-mail: sales@jplfulfillment.com
Tel: 877.683.6935

First published 2014

British Library Cataloguing in Publication Data available
ISBN: 978-085234-960-1

Unless otherwise indicated, all Scripture quotations are from the Holy Bible, Authorized (King James) Version.

Contents

Preface

For over fifty years I have been using the books of J. A. Alexander. The first of them was his commentary on the Psalms, which I used in 1959. It was also the first of his books I actually owned. When I was working on a Th.M thesis on the Book of Acts under Dr N. B. Stonehouse at Westminster Theological Seminary during 1961–62, I acquired a copy of his commentary on that book. Over the years I have obtained all his major books, and my appreciation of him and his work has grown. He was a brilliant, though unusual, scholar. In this book I try to paint the picture of his life and work, and also an assessment of his significance.

I thank my wife, Mairi, for her continued help in my ministry. I am also grateful for the assistance of a friend, John Cromarty, who read over my manuscript.

Allan M. Harman

Timeline

1809	Born in Philadelphia, USA, on 24 April 1809
1812	His father, Archibald Alexander, appointed as the first professor of Princeton Theological Seminary, and the family move to Princeton
1826	Graduated with the B.A. degree from the College of New Jersey (now Princeton University)
1830	Appointed as Adjunct Professor of Ancient Languages and Literature in the College of New Jersey
1833–34	European tour and study
1834–38	Assistant to Charles Hodge in the Oriental Department at Princeton Seminary
1838	Appointed Adjunct Professor of Oriental and Biblical Literature

1840	Appointed the Professor of Oriental and Biblical Literature
1846–47	Commentary on Isaiah published
1850	Commentary on Psalms published
1851	Transferred to the chair of Biblical and Ecclesiastical History
1856	Commentary of Acts published
1858	Commentary on Mark published
1859	Transferred to the chair of Hellenistic and New Testament Literature
1860	Died and was buried at Princeton
1860	Posthumous publication of his two volumes of sermons, *Sermons, Joseph Addison Alexander, D.D.* (republished in 2004 with the title, *Theology on Fire: Sermons from the Heart of J. A. Alexander*)
1861	Posthumous publication of his commentary on Matthew 1-16
1867	Posthumous publication of his book, *Notes on the New Testament and Ecclesiastical History*

1.
Family background and early life in Princeton

In 1812, a young Joseph Addison Alexander (1809–1860), just three years old, moved to Princeton, New Jersey, when his father, Dr Archibald Alexander (1772–1851), accepted appointment by the General Assembly of the Presbyterian Church of America as the first professor in a new seminary. Princeton was only a small town of about 3,000 people when the seminary began. Though the choice of Princeton was at first considered temporary, just a year after its foundation the General Assembly confirmed that it was the permanent site, and building work got underway on the first of the seminary buildings.

Joseph had been born on 24 April 1809, but from early childhood his family called him by his second name, Addison. From the age of three Princeton was his home until his death, except for the period he spent in Europe in 1833–34 and the later shorter visit in the summer of 1853.

During that time it increased greatly in size. Whereas at an early period there was no direct link between Princeton and the main railway system, a branch line was later built, and connections with major centres like Philadelphia and New York became much easier.

Princeton was well known as it had been the site of the Princeton College since 1746. Early American Presbyterian ministers were usually prepared for ministry by living and studying with an experienced pastor. Some of these pastors became known for having the skills to prepare young men for pastoral work, and often trained several at the same time. In 1727 William Tennent Sr (1673–1746) established an academy on the Little Neshaminy Creek in Bucks County, Pennsylvania, that came to be called the Log College. George Whitefield (1714–1770), on his second visit to America, visited it in 1739, and commented that seven or eight young men had just been sent forth, with more students almost ready to enter the ministry. The Log College closed in 1742, but students from it had started similar academies. Discussions were held about establishing a more permanent institution, especially when Yale College showed itself very unfriendly to those who supported the Great Awakening. David Brainerd (1718–1747), the missionary to the Indians, was expelled from there for his 'intemperate, indiscrete zeal'.

While not an official Presbyterian Church establishment, all the early trustees of the College of New Jersey at Princeton were either Presbyterian ministers or elders. Its aim was twofold. On the one hand it was to train men for the ministry, while on the other hand it was envisaged as a place where others would be trained for various useful professions. While it began in the manse of Rev. Jonathan Dickinson (1688–1747) of Elizabethtown, New Jersey, it was moved to Princeton in 1756. Its first buildings were largely paid for by donations received in Britain on a deputation visit by Revs Gilbert Tennent (1703–1764) and Samuel Davies (1723–1761) two years previously. Of the early presidents, five died in the first twenty years of its existence, including Jonathan Edwards (1703–1758), who succeeded his son-in-law, Aaron Burr (1716–1757). Edwards died after a smallpox vaccination in March 1758, having only begun his duties in January of that year.

After two short presidencies, John Witherspoon (1723–1794), minister of the Church of Scotland in Paisley, was invited to accept the position. The trustees were not put off by his refusal of the first invitation, and after two years he was prevailed upon to accept, arriving with his family in August 1768. He had a distinguished career there, but was also very involved in the affairs of the Presbyterian Church and in national politics. He took a very pro-active role on the republican side, and was one of the fifty-five men who signed the Declaration of Independence in 1776.

Witherspoon himself taught many classes at the college, including the languages — Greek, Hebrew, Latin and French. He also lectured in moral philosophy and divinity. His influence on many of the young men was profound, with 114 of his former students becoming Presbyterian ministers. But this influence was not to last. He died in 1794, and was succeeded by his son-in-law, Samuel Smith. However, the ethos of the college was changing, and no longer did it blend scientific and religious teaching in such a way that it prepared men for the ministry. While the college had about 200 students, very few of them were ministerial candidates. At one time over half of the graduates of the college went into the Presbyterian ministry, but by the early 1800s only 9% did so, in spite of the fact that a Presbyterian minister was the full-time professor of theology.

About 1800, Ashbel Green (1762–1848), the pastor of Second Presbyterian Church in Philadelphia, started speaking to others about the possibility of the Presbyterian Church establishing its own seminary, independent of Princeton College. He spoke at a later assembly about the shortage of ministers, and the outcome was that there was a call to presbyteries to work for an increase in the number of candidates and to provide them with adequate support. The General Assembly in 1809 sent out to presbyteries a proposal with three options: a single seminary, one in the south with another in the north, or a seminary in every synod. The majority favoured the first option, and it became the one that carried. A plan, largely the work of Ashbel Green, was prepared, and it envisaged godly staff committed to the Scriptures and the doctrinal standards of the church that would train students not only academically, but in real godliness.

At the 1812 Assembly the decision was made that Princeton was to be the location of the seminary. A board consisting of twenty-one ministers and nine elders was elected, and then after prayer, Dr Archibald Alexander was elected as the first professor. He regretted leaving his congregation in Philadelphia, and thought that he was unqualified for the task. However, he responded to the call of the church and concurred in the decision. There was only one Presbyterian

Church in Princeton, a brick one built in 1760, having fifty-seven pews and galleries on three sides. It was full on 12 August 1812 as Archibald Alexander was installed. He gave a lengthy address on John 5:39: 'Search the Scriptures'. By the next year, Archibald Alexander was joined by a colleague, Samuel Miller (1769–1850). Alexander and Miller had first met at the General Assembly in Philadelphia in 1801, Miller serving in a collegial ministry in the Presbyterian Church of New York. The collegiate was broken up in 1809, and Miller became the pastor of the Wall Street Presbyterian Church. While Alexander was appointed to teach theology, Miller was the professor of Ecclesiastical History and Church Government. These two men were dominant in the life of Princeton Seminary for over thirty years, with Alexander dying in 1850 and Miller in 1851.

Archibald Alexander was minister of Third Presbyterian Church in Philadelphia when his appointment was made. At that church he ministered to a large congregation, especially of Scots/Irish artisans. He was a southerner, from Virginia, being born seven miles east of Lexington, where his Scottish-Irish grandparents had come after first migrating from Ulster to Pennsylvania. It was a hard life on the frontier, and his grandmother was killed by Indians. At an early age he had to learn how to ride a horse and to shoot.

While Archibald Alexander's grandfather had been converted during the Great Awakening, his father, though a Presbyterian elder, did not show the same spirituality. After schooling under William Graham in Hanover County, Alexander served as a tutor in the home of General John Posey in Fredericksburg. One Sunday night he was reading from John Flavel's writings at the request of a godly woman who was part of a group at General Posey's. As he read, his emotions became too stirred, and he broke off the reading. He then went to his room and dropped on his knees seeking mercy from the Lord.

He studied again under William Graham along with several other ministerial candidates, and was licensed in October 1791 at the age of nineteen. For three years he served as an itinerant evangelist, preaching simple sermons to country folk. One man in an obscure place paid him a great compliment when, after listening to him, said, 'I guess he aint a very *larned* man!' During this period he preached effectively without notes and decided to carry on in this way. After serving in southern Virginia and as president of the recently commenced Hampden-Sydney College, Archibald Alexander moved to Pine Street Church in Philadelphia in 1807. This church was also known as Third Presbyterian Church. Believing this was God's call, he went, but was never attracted to the sophisticated social life or the crowded city conditions.

The Archibald Alexander family consisted of seven children, six sons and one daughter. The family had to get used to the busy and varied life of their father as he had many responsibilities in the early years of the seminary's existence. His own modest home at first was the library, chapel and classroom, with students participating in meals and family worship. His wife, Janetta, shared her husband's religious convictions. She encouraged him when he was downcast, was a mother to her own children, an 'elder sister' to read the religious books she had grown to love in her childhood home, and was able to explain the Scriptures very well. In fact, Addison Alexander once said that if he was working on a difficult verse of Scripture, he would go and ask his mother for her opinion, which 'was worth more than all the commentaries in the world.'

Though Archibald Alexander was very busy, his children were always allowed access to him, except at times of devotion. They were allowed to go in and out of his study, have their books and toys on the floor, and no matter what noise they made, he was undisturbed. The older children went to school, but for much of their education their father was the teacher. He himself could read the New Testament when he was six years old, and at seven he had memorized the *Westminster Shorter Catechism.* As soon as the children could read English words, he started to give them Latin words and their meaning to memorize. It wasn't long before Addison knew 1000 Latin words. In addition to biblical knowledge, Archibald encouraged them with spelling, geography, arithmetic and algebra.

Addison was taught to read by a young lady who was living with the family, and from then on he read incessantly. By the time he was about six he would go to the kitchen every night after the evening meal. There he would read aloud from Bunyan's *Pilgrim's Progress* to an old Negro cook. He would even stop now and then and explain what he had read. As for writing, he had taught himself to do so before the others in the family were aware of it.

His father sensed that Addison was different from the other children, and decided that he would give him his early education at home. He realized that he had exceptional ability with languages, and when he was six years old, he wrote out for him the Hebrew alphabet and then later followed this up with a manuscript on Hebrew grammar. The title page read:

HEBREW GRAMMAR,
WITH THE POINTS,
Translated from Leusden's
Compend of Buxtorf,
FOR JOSEPH ADDISON ALEXANDER

Princeton, New Jersey,
A.D. 1819

Addison had other interests as well. He taught himself to play an improvised flute made from a bamboo cane. Later he was given, first, a small flute, and later a larger one. He studied and copied music. But this music was not for the entertainment of others. It was simply for his own enjoyment, and though his brother James played the flute well, no one could recall them playing together. From the age of seven he wrote poetry, though he laughingly didn't regard those poems as of high quality. Once he commented that William Cowper was regarded as a great poet because he never published any of the poems he wrote in his youth! Other members of the family were very bright also. Archibald Alexander wrote to his sister and mentioned James, William and Addison.

> *Addison is also learning Latin, and greatly exceeds all our other children in capacity. He does not equal James in quickness, nor William in memory; but in the clearness of his*

> *ideas, and his steely attention to whatever he undertakes to study, he is greatly superior to them both. He has written several poems, but they are not worth sending so far.*

Before he went to a school, he was reading English, Latin and Hebrew. He had also started learning Greek, though the family could not be sure when he started it. His first teacher outside his family was James Hamilton, who drilled him in mathematics, and while he was good at it, his interests lay in other directions. For a time, somewhere around 1816 or 1817, he went to a school run by Dr Lindsley, the Vice-President of Princeton College, at which he was taught by Salmon Strong. Afterwards, when a boy of nine or ten years of age, he attended small classes taught by Horace Pratt. By 1819 he was studying French under the tutelage of Robert Baird, a first-year student at the seminary, who also spent an hour each afternoon teaching Greek to Addison and his older brother William. Baird afterwards was head of a new academy started in Princeton that Addison attended. While a student there, he also taught for an hour every morning and afternoon, and when doing so, no trace of his natural diffidence was apparent. If he came to school early, a crowd soon gathered around him. Addison was continuing to read widely and at this time even ran a weekly hand-written journal.

In 1823, when Addison was thirteen, his father wrote to a family friend, detailing some of his studies. His son was studying fourteen hours a day, had no desire to be a teacher, and was delighting in a couple of Persian manuscripts he had found in the college library. He was even writing in Arabic, for a manuscript survived that had the inscription:

An Arabic translation of the title-page of 'Waverley', by Jos. A. Alexander. Princeton, August 20, 1822.

At this stage his father thought that 'unless the grace of God prevent', Addison would probably pursue a course in law. How delighted the father was later when God's grace did intervene, and Addison ultimately joined him on the faculty of the seminary.

At the age of fifteen Addison commenced studying at Princeton College. Because of his superior educational attainments he was able to join the Junior class (i.e., the third-year class), and so was only enrolled as a student for two years before he graduated with a B.A. degree in 1826. Many of his fellow students realized some of his amazing abilities, not only in languages, but in history and literature. One, later a judge, thought that his imagination, if given free rein, would have produced wonderful, popular literature. His father recognized that his son was exceptional, and when writing to a friend he commented that Addison was 'very far superior to anyone of his age I ever saw in literary attainments'. However, he was extremely reticent to speak about religious topics, and the family did not know where he really stood in spiritual matters.

James and Addison were very close as brothers. Their nephew, Henry Carrington Alexander, said that in a sense Addison had no friend other than James. The only close associate was Rezeau Brown, who started studying Hebrew with him in 1828 and then became a tutor at Princeton College before entering Princeton Seminary as a student. His friendship with James and Addison was strong, and Rezeau assisted James for a time in editorial work in connection with the *Presbyterian*, a religious paper he was editing. Rezeau was to accompany Addison on his trip to Europe in 1833, but ill-health prevented this from happening. While Addison mixed with others at college, he preferred to be alone or with James, and when James died, Addison was inconsolable, dying shortly afterwards himself. Addison's reputation spread, and a fellow student later called him 'a studious recluse.' Many knew about him, not because of personal contact, but because he was contributing to papers, or speaking at meetings of the Philological Society at the college. He normally ate after the rest of the family, and while he didn't seek out company, he did take part readily in conversation with any visitors to the home.

Even before he finished at the college, his linguistic and other gifts were recognized. He was known to contribute to a weekly hand-written newspaper in Princeton. It was called the *New Jersey Patriot*, and for a time he and one of his brothers were the editors. When he was only seventeen, he wrote an article for it on Persian poetry that attracted attention. About that time he also wrote for a short-lived paper in Philadelphia called the *Souvenir*, and then for the *Philadelphia Monthly Magazine*. Some of his contributions were prose, others poetry. After reading Genesis 27 in Hebrew, and especially Esau's pathetic appeal to his father for a blessing, he composed a long poem in blank verse called 'The Tears of Esau.'

A new printing press was established in Princeton in 1824, and in the following year Charles Hodge inaugurated the *Biblical Repertory*. His intention was to create a new journal that was 'designed to render accessible to American readers some of the fruits of the mature learning of English and German scholars'. When Addison Alexander was only seventeen, he contributed his first article. This was a translation of a discussion by Jean Alphonso Turretin (1671–1737) entitled 'Refutation of the Hypothesis of the Papists in Relation to the Interpretation of the Scriptures'. In Boston people talked about this article and thought it was from the pen of Addison's father, Archibald Alexander. It was followed by another article, a translation of Justin Martyr's 'Exhortation to the Greeks' that also involved translation of classical authors to whom reference was made. This early involvement was the start of a long connection with the *Biblical Repertory*, which changed its name first to *Biblical Repertory and Theological Review*, and then to *Biblical Repertory and Princeton Review*. At the age of nineteen he was clearly assisting in some way, for he noted in his diary that he had been to consult Charles Hodge about proof sheets for the *Repertory*.

By the time he had graduated from college, he was already a linguist of remarkable note. In addition to Latin and Greek he was working at Hebrew, Syriac, Arabic, Persian, French, German and Italian. His diary for early 1828 shows how diligent he was in his linguistic study. Here are two examples:

> *Jan. 1.—Arabic. Al Koran, Sura. 19. Hebrew, Exodus, chap. xix. Italian, Tasso [Italian poet 1544-1595], Ger. Lib. [La Gerursaliemma liberata, 'Jerusalem Delivered'] Canto 12, Latin, Cicero in Q. Caecillium, German, Rules of pronunciation; Greek, Matthew, chaps. 1-4.*

Jan. 5.— Hebrew, Exod. Chs. 22-23. Arabic, Al Koran, Suras 20-21. Latin, Cicero Orat. Pro Lege Manilla. Greek, Matt. Chs. 17-20. French, Description de l'Arabe, par Niebuhr. English, Byron's poems. Italian, wrote translation of Historia Sacra. German, wrote paradigms of ten auxiliary verbs.

He was in the custom of summarizing on the last day of the month what he had achieved in linguistic studies during that month. On 31 January 1828 he wrote:

During the month which is now closing, I have read thirty-two chapters in the Hebrew Bible, all of them twice and most of them three times; seventeen Suras [sections] in the Koran — all of them twice except the first and the last. I have also, within this month, begun the study of the German language, and made such progress as shall be mentioned hereafter. I commenced reading the Greek Testament on the first of the month, but discontinued it after finishing two gospels. On the 11th inst. I commenced the practice of repeating what I had read in Hebrew in Martini's Italian version, which I have regularly continued. On the 25th inst. I procured the 5th volume of Walton's Polyglot, *and since that date, have read the Scriptures in six languages on the following plan. 1. Leviticus in the morning; in Hebrew critically, (i.e. with grammar and lexicon). 2. The Gospel of John in the morning in German — critically; at night in Spanish cursorily. 3. The Gospel of Matthew in the morning in Persian — critically; at night, in Arabic cursorily; repeating every day the readings of the preceding. These readings I have, since the 25th, been my standing orders of the day, which I was not at liberty to set aside. My moveable orders of the day, which might be dispensed with, if necessary or shifted from one day to*

> *another, were—1. The critical reading of Don Quixote in Spanish. 2. The reading of the Telemaque in French. 3. All English reading; and lastly, composition. On Sundays I have been in the practice of repeating the portions of Scripture read during the week.*

While Addison Alexander had written many journal or newspaper articles, his first book was on sacred geography. It is unclear whether he approached the American Sunday School Union, or if it approached him, though the latter is more likely. He was already working on it in June 1829, basing it on the German one of similar intent by E. F. C. Rosenmüller (1768–1835). About half way through his work, he became 'disgusted' with it and passed over to his brother James the responsibility of finishing it. James reported progress in a letter to Addison on 2 September 1829, requesting that Addison, not withstanding his 'disgust', should finish the section on Phœnicia. James could also point to errors in some of the books he was using. Mansford had published a book called *The Scripture Gazeteer*, but, James asserted, wherever he was strictly original he was wrong! Rosenmüller could also be mistaken on points, such as asserting that Gamaliel had a school at Tarsus, whereas Paul says that he was brought up at the feet of Gamaliel '*in this city*' (Acts 22:3), i.e., in Jerusalem. Soon James sent some of the manuscript to Addison, and took the rest in person; and Addison proceeded to read and correct it. The book was finally finished and published the following year.

Even James found some of the work on it tiresome. In a letter of 14 September 1829 he wrote:

> *Addison has consigned to me his papers and notes on Sacred Geography, and I have been engaged in finishing the book, so that we shall have it between us. The labour has been very irksome. I spent twelve hours last week verifying the texts of Scripture referred to, by looking for all of them. The mere geographical part is very interesting. Altogether it is discouraging to find how little is really known of the site of many ancient places.*

This book was a first in America. It drew upon discoveries made by recent travellers to the Near East, and on views expressed by commentators. It was a considerable achievement for the two young brothers and amounted to 180 pages. While the largest part of the book was devoted to Palestine, a good coverage was given to all the regional areas mentioned in the biblical text. No maps were provided. Soon after its publication, other books of this nature were published, written by those who had seen the Near East for themselves. Edward Robinson (1794–1863) of Andover and Union Seminaries travelled widely in the Holy Land in 1837–39 and identified more biblical sites than anyone since Eusebius of Caesarea (*c.* 265 - *c.* 340). His book, *Biblical Researches in Palestine, Mount Sinai and Arabea Petraea*, was published in 1840. No mention is made by Addison Alexander of any attempt by him to travel to Palestine and see for himself the biblical sites, and so have first-hand acquaintance with the geography and history of the Near East. In fact, as late as 1890–93 when George L. Robinson (1864–1954), later of McCormick Seminary, Chicago, was a student at the seminary, none of the eight professors had visited the Near East. Robinson had just spent three years teaching in Lebanon, and had travelled widely throughout the region including in Lebanon, Palestine and Egypt. This lack of firsthand knowledge of Palestine by the faculty says something about the orientation of teaching at Princeton in the nineteenth century at least.

After a period of extended private study, in 1829 Addison taught for some time at a school run by himself and Professor Patton. He taught Latin, geography, ancient and modern history, and English composition. While other students walked along the banks of streams near Princeton, Addison, though he sometimes went for a walk, found recreation in his books, or else in entertaining children. He was building up his own library, but other sources were near at hand. He could go to his father's library, or borrow from his brother, James, or search in the seminary and college libraries, though no borrowing was allowed from the institutional libraries.

2.

Early spiritual experiences

It was while he was teaching at Professor Patton's school that Addison had a real spiritual change. Up to this time he was outwardly religious, practically never absent from the daily opening and closing prayer and Scripture reading at the Academy. He attended the prayer meeting on Tuesday afternoon and the Bible class on Sunday afternoon. But then a change came early in 1830 when he was twenty years of age. Fortunately, his spiritual diary for this period survived up to the day after his twenty-first birthday on 24 April. From that point onwards there is little about his spiritual condition or feelings, because he wrote of such things in a separate diary that was afterwards destroyed.

In January 1830 he was very busy with his linguistic and literary pursuits. He was helping Professor Patton in collecting entries for the Greek lexicon on which he was working, as well as finishing a notice on a book for the *American Quarterly Review*, and some short pieces for the

Philadelphia Morning Journal. Then came a very significant entry in his diary:

> *But in addition to these literary pursuits, I have been deeply engaged in a study new to me, and far more important than all others — the study of the Bible and my own heart. I humbly trust that I am not what I was. I have still my old propensities to evil, but I have also a new will co-existing with the old, and counteracting and controlling it. My views respecting study are now changed. Intellectual enjoyment has been my idol heretofore; now my heart's desire is that I may live no longer to myself, but to Him in whom I have everlasting life. God grant that the acquisitions that I have been allowed to make under the influence of such selfish motives may be turned to good account as instruments for the promotion of His glory.*

This diary entry is important on two counts. First, it marks the spiritual change that came at this time in his life. The student scholar now had another interest. His heart and life were changed, much to the delight of his father. An account of a conversation between Robert Baird, one of Addison's early tutors, and Archibald Alexander makes reference to his conversion. This is what Baird wrote:

> *After speaking of the business respecting which I had called to see him, he remarked that as I had taken a great interest in his sons, he had a piece of intelligence to communicate which he was sure would give me much delight. He then stated that he was well satisfied, from a conversation which he had with Addison the evening previous, that he was a converted man! This he said in a tone of voice which*

> *manifested the deepest feeling. Indeed, for some moments afterwards he could not speak, but covered his face with his handkerchief, and gave way to his deep emotions of joy and hope.*

It is probable that Addison is referring to the same conversation when he made his diary entry on 4 February 1830. He noted that he had 'been suffering the pains of melancholy' [depression], though he added that he was tempted to believe 'that it is a device of the adversary intended to throw a shade over the subject of religion, and alienate my thoughts from it.' To this he added: 'I was somewhat relieved by conversing with my father last night, but find myself still under the dominion of evil spirits, especially as night comes on.' This daily variation in feelings while suffering from depression is well known.

The second important thing is that this experience brought about a marked changed in his reading and his general outlook on his studies. In addition to his notes on language study, his diary contains reference to wider theological and biblical reading. He read abridgements of Edwards on the *Affections* and the life of Henry Martyn. He commented on the epistles of Peter, Romans 8, and the book of Ecclesiastes. In a single week he read forty-four chapters of the English Bible, and while finishing his reading of the Greek text of Matthew he also read all of Mark and eight chapters of Luke in Greek. His interests were moving from merely secular study to biblical and theological. On 24 April he noted that it was his twenty-first birthday, and the change in his spiritual state is very apparent from the entry. Here is a section of it:

> *I am this day twenty-one years old, and after looking upon my past life, and forward to eternity, having also sought instruction from God's Word and at the throne of grace, I desire with few words, but with a fixed heart, to consecrate myself, soul and body, now and forever, to the God who made me. With this intent I now most solemnly renounce the service of the devil, my late master; abandoning not only certain sins, but* sin *itself; with all its pleasures, honours and emoluments; desiring and beseeching God never more to suffer me to taste the least enjoyment of a sinful nature. I also bind my conscience in the presence of the jealous God who searches the heart and cannot look upon iniquity without abhorrence, to watch against all temptation; and if necessary, to resist unto blood striving against sin.*

Temptations constantly came to him. He found himself lacking assurance, first of all concerning the truth of Christianity, and then assurance of his own personal interest in Christ. The temptations, he realized, were not only external to himself, but in his own heart. If he tried to reason his way through the temptations, all arguments failed. He asked himself the question: 'What then is to sustain me?' He answered:

> *The grace of God imparted at the moment and proportioned to the exigency. How is it to be had? By prayer and holy living through the Saviour's intercession. How shall I be assured of having it in season? Trust — trust — trust in God. Remember that you do not deserve to be sustained at all; that if you are, it is a mere favour. What assurance, then is wanting but a knowledge of God's goodness and a firm faith in his promises?*

At this period he continued his linguistic studies, starting on Danish and Turkish. He pursed general reading on literature and philosophy, and wrote some articles for the *Philadelphia Morning Journal*. While he read quite widely in philosophy, it was clearly not his first interest. Much later, Dr Charles Hodge, in an address given at the reopening of the seminary chapel in 1874, said of Addison Alexander, 'If, when reading a book he came across any philosophical discussion, he would turn over the leaves until he found more congenial matter.'

In July 1830 Addison suffered from scarlet fever, and as he recovered, he was appointed Adjunct Professor of Ancient Languages and Literature in the College of New Jersey, a position he held until he left for Europe about two and a half years later. While the regularity of his work was congenial, the routines seemed to bore him, as he was exhibiting a tendency, very marked later in life, of liking frequent change — in his accommodation and work. This was also the period when he finally decided to study for the ministry. He set himself to work for three days in the week on biblical studies, reading books on biblical criticism under the guidance of his friend and mentor, Charles Hodge. He sought advice from his father as to subjects he should work on, and attended lectures his father was giving to the seminary students on metaphysics. Two days a week were devoted to systematic theology, and one day to history. Sunday, the Lord's Day, was solely given over to biblical reading and books on Christian living. This general pattern he followed right through 1831 and 1832.

One isolated reference in his journal notes something of his spiritual battles. He read the life of the Scottish theologian,

Thomas Halyburton (1674–1712), a writer that his father had read soon after his conversion in 1788. Surprisingly, he found that Halyburton and himself shared almost identical spiritual experiences up to the age of twenty. Both were sons of Presbyterian ministers, and both outwardly lived respectable lives before their spiritual awakening. He learned a lot from this biography and especially that when he sinned, he had to look to Christ's atonement as the source of forgiveness.

The intensity of his studies amazes a modern reader. During the early part of 1832 he read the prophecy of Isaiah in eight languages — Hebrew, Aramaic, Syriac, Greek, Latin, English, Arabic and German. At the same time, among other things, he was working his way through Horne's *Introduction* to the Scriptures, Paley on both *Natural Theology* and *Evidences,* Moses Stuart on the Epistle to the Hebrews, Bush on the *Millenium,* and his father's work on the canon of Scripture. When he heard his father speak at a Sunday afternoon conference about storing Scripture in the memory, Addison began to memorize the whole of the Psalter in English and Hebrew, and the first few verses of each chapter of Isaiah. To his students at the college, he was lecturing in Greek, while teaching German and French to one of his brothers, and two young ladies.

3.
Study in Europe

Addison Alexander was mentored by Charles Hodge (1797–1878), who was over eight years his senior. Hodge had lost his father when he was very young, and Archibald Alexander almost assumed the role of father to him. Later he testified that he was 'moulded more by the character and instructions of Dr Archibald Alexander, than by all other external influences combined.' Hodge had joined the staff of the seminary in May 1820 when he was appointed on a one-year contract to be an assistant, teaching the original languages of Scripture. He carried out this task so well that he was elected Professor of Oriental and Biblical Literature in 1821. The idea of Addison spending time in Europe probably came about because of Hodge's study there from October 1826 until September 1828. His family and friends encouraged him to travel and to see many places he had read about and also to make contact with places of higher learning. His friend Rezeau Brown was to accompany him, but illness prevented him, and later, while in Italy, Addison heard the news of his death.

On the 10 April 1833 he sailed from New York. When the ship arrived at Portsmouth, he took the stagecoach to London, delighting in the scenery: 'little gardens, exquisitely neat, grass-plots of the most delicious green, hedges and trees and shrubbery.' The horses were changed six or seven times, and the roadway must have been fairly good, for Alexander said that 'the motion of the coach was all but imperceptible'! In London he listened to a debate in the House of Commons and indulged his interest in legal matters by going to the High Court of Chancery. Having heard of Rev. Edward Irving (1792–1834) and his eccentric ministry, he decided to go and hear him. In a letter home he described the church in Newman Street, how Irving was dressed, and the very disorganized worship that he witnessed. When Irving spoke or prayed, his voice was harsh, but like a trumpet. While one elder spoke more than once in an unknown language, others addressed the congregation on subjects like faith, or union with Christ. His verdict on Irving was this: 'Everything that fell from Irving's lips was purely flat and stupid, without a single flash of genius, or the slightest indication of strength of even vivacity of mind. I was confirmed in my former low opinion of him founded on his writings.'

After visiting Oxford he went north by coach to Edinburgh, describing the coachman as a perfect Jehu. From a distance he saw the spires of Auld Reekie and commented that he felt at that moment he was in another world. He delighted in the castle, the splendid churches, and the lofty range of stone buildings. John Knox's house was marked by an inscription, but occupied at that time by a fashionable hairdresser and wigmaker.

On the Continent he enjoyed Paris. There he was able to visit the aged General Lafayette (1757–1834), who had served notably in the American War of Independence, and from him he received letters of introduction to some important places and people. On Sunday he heard an English sermon in the morning, but at night he listened at the Oratoire to a fine sermon in French from Adolf Monod (1802–1856) on the introduction to the Lord's Prayer and on the first clause. From Paris he moved on to Munich, Berne, Lausanne and Geneva. Monod had provided him with letters of introduction, including one to the historian, Dr Merle D'Aubigné (1794–1872). He proceeded down through Italy to Rome, noting that he escaped any customs examination because one of his travelling companions was a kind, but unscrupulous, old Catholic bishop.

By the middle of October 1833, he was in Halle where he stayed till the end of the year. There his Continental studies really began. Charles Hodge had given him a letter of introduction to Professor Freidrich Tholuck (1799–1877), and Addison was often in his company, including going on walks with him. He listened to other professors and also met Pastor Rudolph Stier (1800–1862), author of a well-known book entitled *The Words of Jesus*. He even noted the attendance at lectures. One day Tholuck had a hundred present, Fuch on Genesis fifteen, while Pott on Sanscrit only had four. When not at lectures he continued his normal programme of biblical reading — Numbers, Judges, Isaiah and Ecclesiastes in Hebrew, and Matthew, 1 Corinthians, Acts and Revelation in Greek. He was always looking around the bookshops and bought books on German philosophy as well as those on Semitic languages. Clearly he was able to converse well in German, though an American friend there at the same time said that while his own German was meagre and conversational, Addison's was 'copious, but labored, being manufactured on the spot from the grammar and the dictionary'. He also recorded how Addison, when moving to a new country, would go into a restaurant and at random order from the menu. When it came, he knew what it was! He was caught out by this once when the waiter brought him a huge crab, which he paid for but did not eat.

From Halle he moved on to Berlin in early January 1836. Immediately he was in touch with Professor E. W. Hengtensberg (1802–1869) and commenced attending his exposition of Hosea. The lectures were in Latin. This was the start of an important relationship between Addison Alexander and Hengstenberg, though he was not afraid to differ from his mentor. He attended the French church on Sunday and also the Domkirche, where on one occasion he heard David Strauss (1808–1874) preach upon the Gospel passage of the day, Matthew 3. He also heard one of the last lectures of Friedrich Scheiermacher (1768–1834) on the final words of 1 Peter, and about a week later learned that he had died from an inflammation of the lungs. Scheiermacher partook of communion, and then repeated the *Apostles' Creed*, adding, 'In this faith I die'. His last words were '*Die Barmherzigkeit Gottes*' ('the mercy of God').

His time in Berlin was just as busy as the other centres he had visited. He commenced study of Rabbinic or post-biblical Hebrew, attended a wide variety of lectures, and visited quite a number of the professors in their own homes, with the conversations sometimes being in English, at other times in German. However, even while busy with all these activities, he kept up many of his other scholarly pursuits and recorded in his diary his readings in Hebrew, Greek and medieval Jewish authors.

After two months in Berlin, Alexander moved on in early March 1834 to the final stage of his European experience. Even during a brief stay in Göttingen he was able to hear the famous Old Testament scholar, Georg Ewald (1803–1875), lecture on biblical history. From there he went via Frankfurt on Main and Coblenz to Bonn. It took him a further week to reach Paris, using the renewed opportunity of a stay there to visit interesting places and sites, before heading for Le Havre. He sailed on the ship *Poland*, and it took a month to reach New York. Never idle, he read a lot on the voyage, including Arabic, as an acquaintance recorded.

4.
Early teaching at Princeton Seminary

The young scholar, after the stimulus of his European experiences, returned to Princeton in May 1834. While he was abroad, the seminary board had elected him as Adjunct Professor of Oriental Literature. He declined this appointment, though willingly became Charles Hodge's assistant, while also teaching again at Edgehill School for about sixteen hours per week. The connection with Princeton Seminary was to continue without interruption until his death in 1860.

The time when Addison Alexander returned to Princeton was a period of tension within the Presbyterian Church, and though he did not take any real part in the public discussions, he followed them with great interest. Presbyterianism came to the United States in two waves. The first was with the early Puritan settlements in New England, while the second was the Scottish-Irish migration in the seventeenth century. Colonial presbyteries were established early in the eighteenth century, and the first General Assembly of the Presbyterian Church in the United States met in 1789.

Two major issues developed over the decades, and they came to a climax in the 1830s. The Presbyterian Church had become divided into Old School and New School adherents. The first issue concerned different viewpoints on subscription to the *Westminster Confession of Faith*. The New Englanders were regarded as holding to a loose subscription, as their position, at least in the eyes of their opponents, had been influenced by revivalism. They seemed more preoccupied with personal piety than with strict subscription to doctrinal statements. On the other hand the Scottish-Irish ministers were more doctrinally oriented and held stricter views on church order.

The second issue was somewhat related to the first in that revivalist movements stressed the personal relationship of the sinner to Christ and even considered that the Calvinistic message of the *Westminster Confession of Faith* was a hindrance, if not directly antithetical to evangelism. Charles Finney (1792–1875), though a Presbyterian minister, took over evangelistic methods already practised by the Methodists, and his theology was really Arminian, not Calvinist. The doctrinal changes in the church were marked by a considerable number of people leaving to join professedly Arminian churches, or to share in the formation of the Cumberland Presbyterian Church in 1808 that had a distinctly Arminian theology.

The Princeton faculty members were closest to the Old School, though they were more mediating than many others. While other faculty members, such as Samuel Miller, tried to pacify both sides and so avoid a split in the denomination, Archibald Alexander and Charles Hodge were active in the General Assembly and in their writings defending the Old School position. Strength of the two opposing parties in the General Assembly oscillated during the 1830s until finally, in 1837, with the Old School in the majority, the General Assembly took action that caused the break to occur. The Plan of Union of 1801 that sanctioned Congregational-Presbyterian cooperation in church planting was overturned, for the Old School men believed that this had enabled New England theology that was antithetical to the Calvinism of the *Westminster Confession of Faith* to come into the Presbyterian Church. Several synods were also expelled, particularly those in western New York. The end result was the division of the church into two almost equal sections, Old School and New School. The support of Princeton Seminary for the Old School had consequences, for the student numbers dropped, and financial support was greatly reduced for a time.

Many of Addison Alexander's characteristics were clear from this period. He had to be constantly moving his place of abode, and if this didn't happen, he was changing the position of the books in his study. Unless he was busy, he seemed unhappy. He even varied the way in which he prepared his manuscripts, using different shapes and sizes of paper. One acquaintance told how he had seen one of his manuscripts on which the written lines were running around a large sheet almost in a circle! From his diary entries it is clear that he often worked all day with practically no respite and little food, until he finally noted that he was going to bed.

His amazing memory was always a thing of wonder to students and his faculty colleagues alike. Even when no need existed for memorization, it happened. One of his fellow professors spoke of the procedure at the start of the term. The new students, usually forty or fifty, would matriculate in any order. When the names were needed the next day, Addison would write out the list from memory, even giving their middle initial and classes for which they were enrolled! On the first day of term when meeting his class for the first time, he called out the names of the students in alphabetical order, and each stood up when named. From then on there was no sign of the list, and from memory Addison called on students to participate in the class work.

He was resident in Princeton in winter, though often preaching elsewhere. In summer, he was away on visits, sometimes taking up residence in a hotel in New York in order to get on with his writing. He was very reserved, though in company he could be charming and entertaining. If seminarians were somewhat afraid of him, children were not, and Charles Hodge's son, Archibald Alexander Hodge, used to wrestle with him on the floor, pester him for stories, and listen to him sing in English, French, German, Italian, Turkish, Latin, Greek, Hebrew and Arabic.

Charles Hodge was never reckoned to be a good teacher of Hebrew. On the other hand, Addison Alexander came to the task with a reputation as a brilliant young scholar whom his students found daunting and demanding. He made them work hard, and had little patience with those who were lazy or negligent. Though mellowing later, early on he could be sarcastic and cut down those who were proud or conceited.

If he felt he had acted wrongly, in his next prayer in the Oratory (the prayer hall in the main seminary building) he would display his penitence. A later student said that 'Addison Alexander was undoubtedly the brightest star that ever shone in the Princeton constellation, but he was not the greatest teacher.' The same student also commented that when comparing Moses Stuart (1780–1852) of Andover, Addison Alexander and William Henry Green (1825–1900) as teachers, Green was the greatest because 'talent is better than genius in the class-room.'

He was also ready to further the interests of students in more advanced study of the Old Testament, or to provide the opportunity to learn Arabic or Aramaic. He liked the students to be punctual, and ended the classes precisely on the hour. Quite a few students dropped out of these extra-mural classes, but some continued, several of whom distinguished themselves later as missionaries or seminary teachers.

On his return from Europe he took up again the writing of articles for the *Repertory*. He normally wrote for about an hour at midday, and produced articles on the antiquity of the Pentateuch (based on one of Hengstenberg's studies of the subject), another on the German New Light theology, and a third on the life of Rowland Hill. In addition to his preparation for classes, he was doing his usual biblical reading in Hebrew and Greek, as well as continuing to study Sanscrit and Ethiopic.

In view of his later commentary writing, it is significant that at this time (1834/35) he was lecturing on the prophecy of

Isaiah. Though he only met the second class once a week, he was preparing by reading the ancient and modern versions, together with the commentaries by Chrysostom, Jerome, Theodoret, Jarchi, Eben-Ezra, Kimchi, Calvin, Michaelis, Grotius, Vitringa, Gesenius and Hitzig. It was not till later that he actually started to write his commentary on the book. He was also preparing to lecture on Galilee, and for this he was entering notes in an interleaved copy of the *Geography of Palestine* that he had written with his brother James.

While he had declined the offered appointment as Adjunct Professor of Oriental Literature at the seminary, in May 1835 the General Assembly of the Presbyterian Church elected him to the same position, but again he was unwilling to accept the appointment. When the Board of Directors of the seminary met in September, they had before them a letter from him again declining the position, and saying that he was quite content to remain as an assistant to Professor Charles Hodge. A deputation from the Board met with him, and he consented to defer the matter for twelve months. Others were noting his learning and ability, and the newly formed Union Theological Seminary in New York offered him the professorship in Oriental and Biblical Literature, but he declined.

The 1835 the General Assembly made the significant decision to appoint a Professor of Pastoral Instruction and Missionary Endeavour. The appointee was John Breckenridge (1797–1841), who came from a prominent family. His father had been a senator and attorney-general, but died when his son was only nine years old. He himself had been educated at Princeton College and Princeton Seminary, and was serving as Secretary of the Board of Education in Philadelphia when appointed. He assumed his professorship in May 1836, but only served on the faculty for two years before he resigned to take on the job of secretary to the newly formed Presbyterian Board of Foreign Missions. His appointment was significant in two respects. This was the first time that any seminary had appointed someone to teach specifically in the area of missions. Also, the appointment highlighted for Princeton Seminary the place of mission in the life of the church, and this gave further encouragement to the faculty and students to press on with prayer and practical support for mission work. In the 1830s a number of Princeton graduates went to serve as missionaries, especially to India and Africa. Several of those who went to Africa died tragically from malaria within a very short time. The ethos of the seminary in which the young Addison Alexander was serving had a continuing commitment to evangelical and Reformed theology, but it also had the vision of worldwide evangelization.

An important event for Addison Alexander took place on 21 June 1836 as he recorded in his diary that on that day he began to write his commentary on Isaiah. Because he was lecturing on chapter 49, he started at that point, writing on the first ten verses. He continued to note in his diary his progress with this writing, but also that he was learning Polish with a native speaker, and also looking at Malay and Chinese. In addition some boys used to visit him after school to listen and laugh at his stories.

Becoming a permanent member of the faculty of the seminary was important for him. This led him to reconsider his position in relation to the Presbyterian Church. He approached the Presbytery of New Brunswick in February 1836 seeking to be brought under its care. From a note in his diary for 7 February 1836, it is clear that he had contemplated this move eight years before, which was shortly after his conversion.

In April he was licensed as a preacher of the gospel after he passed his presbyterial exam. A good number of the seminary students were present for this occasion, wanting to see how the presbytery members examined him. What impressed them was not his brilliant answers, but his humility. Sometimes, in response to a question, he simply said, 'I do not know.' This is the way he recorded the event in his diary:

> *I then read my exegesis* De Sacrificis *('Concerning sacrifices'), my critcal exercise on Gen. xlix, 8-12, and my lecture on Micah iv, 1-5; and examined on Theology by Mr Perkins, on Church History by Dr Rice, and on Church Government and the Sacraments by Dr Miller. We then repaired to the church where I delivered my sermon on John iii, 36. Dr Miller and Mr Dod were in the pulpit with me. The latter read the hymns and both made prayers. We then descended from the pulpit. I answered the constitutional questions and was licensed.*

From then on he was in demand as a preacher. His first sermon was in the Princeton church, with many of the faculty and students from both college and seminary present. He showed himself as one who was just as able in the pulpit as he was a professor. His first sermons were well received because of their biblical content, his choice of language, and his evident desire to win souls for the kingdom. When it was reported to his father that he had preached in a large church in New York, his concern was not about the content of the sermon, but whether Addison had spoken loudly enough! Invitations to preach soon multiplied, and this was an increase in his work load in addition to his own study and lecturing. From that point in time he was constantly preaching, especially in New Jersey and in Philadelphia.

This move on his part also led him to reconsider his position in relation to the seminary. The decision of the General Assembly of June 1835, electing him as Adjunct Professor of Oriental and Biblical Literature, still stood. However, it was not till 3 May 1838 that he wrote to the president of the Board of Directors of the seminary, indicating that he would accept the offered professorship. The directors responded by notifying him that he would be inaugurated at their next meeting that was scheduled for September 1838.

That summer saw him moving around a great deal. During the months of April to September he was often away from Princeton, particularly in the corridor between Princeton and New York. Sometimes his visits were extensive; at other times he simply went for rambles. On many occasions he was alone, though on others he was joined by one or other of his brothers. He even reached New England and recorded that on one Sunday he had heard Lyman Beecher (1775–1863) preach twice and gave the texts as, 'Have I any pleasure in the death of the wicked?' and 'Seek first the kingdom of God'. He didn't note any comment on either sermon. His installation as professor took place on 24 September 1838. He had to give an inaugural address and instead of one dealing with Hebrew or Oriental learning, he chose to speak on 'The Scripture

Guide: A Familiar Introduction to the English Bible'. It was really a plea for the study of the English Bible on the same footing as in the original languages. This was an indication of the importance he felt about knowledge and use of the English Bible by pastors. In no way was he disparaging the need for knowledge of the Greek and Hebrew Bibles, but making the practical point that a thorough knowledge of the English Bible was a prerequisite for ministry.

At this time his most frequent companions were his younger brother, Henry Alexander, and Samuel Harrison Howell, a son of the doctor in Princeton, whom he was tutoring. Dr Howell and two others in his family died of a contagious fever, and when Samuel later became ill, Addison wrote him a letter in rhyming prose. In the letter he recounts some of their time together and calls him by his pet name of Hal. Here are some sentences from this letter:

> *I can almost see him still, coming slowly with his books and his umbrella down the hill. Methinks I hear his light step upon the entry floor, and the sound of his umbrella as he sets it by the door. I hear him turn the lock; I see him enter with a smile, my solitude to sweeten and my languor to beguile. Methinks I see him offer me an apple or a peach, with a look that overpays me for the little I can teach. Methinks I see him put his cap upon the closest shelf — every motion, every attitude is that of Hal himself. But when I wish to speak to him the vision fades away. I miss the gentle voice that used to cheer me every day. I miss the real presence of my real little friend. I miss it in the evening when my toils are at an end.*

The first time he preached in the seminary chapel was on 8 December of that year. One of his hearers was Dr Charles Hodge, his mentor from boyhood years and his senior colleague in the Old Testament department. Writing later about Addison Alexander's preaching, he noted that he did not like preaching in the seminary chapel as much as he did to a more general congregation. Also, his preaching there did not have the animation that characterized his sermons elsewhere, thought Hodge.

While Addison Alexander had long been a contributor to the *Biblical Repertory*, in December 1838 he was appointed an editor. At the same time the title was changed with the addition of '*and Princeton Review*'. He was already a prolific contributor, not just on biblical subjects, but also on a wide variety of secular interests.

By 1840 Princeton Seminary was entering a critical period of its history, with several factors combining to initiate change. No longer was it the only Presbyterian seminary. Auburn in the north, Union and Columbia in the south, and Western, Lane and New Albany in the west were all vying for students. Finances continued to be a problem, but a graduate of Princeton, Cortland van Rensselaer, raised $100,000 by 1845 that alleviated that problem. A library building was urgently needed, and this difficulty was solved by the provision of the building as a gift by James Lenox, the son of a Scottish immigrant who had become extremely wealthy through his business dealings in New York City. At first the library had been located in Dr Archibald Alexander's home, then in a second-floor room in the newly constructed seminary building. The holdings in the library were greatly expanded by some notable gifts, such as the collection of twenty thousand pamphlets on early American preaching and religious history that had been gathered by William B. Sprague (1795–1876).

But also pressing was the age of the two founding professors, Archibald Alexander and Samuel Miller. In 1840 Alexander was sixty-eight years of age, while Miller was seventy-one. The solution in relation to Archibald Alexander was the appointment of Charles Hodge, by the General Assembly, as Professor of Exegetical and Didactic Theology. Hodge had not sought this move and was not eager to transfer to another department. However, he yielded to Alexander's wish and began to teach Systematic Theology, though continuing to teach the Pauline epistles to the junior class. The move of Hodge meant that Addison Alexander became the Professor of Biblical and Oriental Literature at the age of thirty-one.

5.
Later Old Testament teaching and preaching ministry

The appointment of Addison Alexander to lead the Old Testament department marked an important milestone in relation to Princeton Seminary. Here was a young man, only ordained two years, who was called on to head an important part of the seminary curriculum. He had the remarkable gifts that had been in evidence right from his early teens, especially in relation to languages. He had spent time in Europe and knew the writings that were coming from scholars who did not share his commitment to the infallibility of Holy Scripture. His teaching was to become an important counterfoil to the critical views that were starting to influence many in America. Alexander respected the scholarship of many of the Continental critics, but was aware that the end result of acceptance of their positions would be disbelief and the abandoning of biblical truth. Also, he had come under the influence of Hengstenberg, and while not always agreeing with him, he certainly disseminated many of his positions to English readers. He had met and admired him while in Germany, but now he became the one who was most prominent in mediating his theological views to American audiences. In the introduction to his volume on the Psalms, he indicated that his first idea was simply to translate Hengstenberg into English.

The early 1840s were extremely busy years for Addison Alexander. It was not until 1847 that he was given assistance in the appointment of William Henry Green as instructor in Hebrew. He carried a full teaching load, was busy with his commentaries on Isaiah and the Psalms, and was also often carrying preaching commitments. For example, in 1847 he took on six months' preaching at Tenth Presbyterian Church in Philadelphia when the pastor, Dr Henry Boardman, was on a trip to Europe. Following that he had a similar appointment for six months at Second Presbyterian Church in Philadelphia. Some of his sermons became well known, and he was often asked to repeat them. One of these was on 'Remember Lot's wife.' Getting weary of this repetition, he said to his brother James, 'I am afraid that woman will be the death of me yet.'

The prodigious learning of Addison Alexander was known far beyond Princeton. Students and visitors carried away with them accounts of his feats of memory, though some stories seem to contain exaggerations. Once, on hearing an incident concerning him recounted, he remarked that it was a case of the rolling stone gathering some moss! In 1844 Rutgers College (now Rutgers University, the state university for New Jersey) conferred on him the honorary degree of D.D. This was on a man of just thirty-five years of age, who, at that time, had published many articles but no major book. He reported in a letter to his and his brother James' mutual friend, Dr John Hall, that when preaching in New York in September 1844 everyone called him 'Doctor'. His attitude to the doctorate comes out in his final sentences: 'Oh, my good sir, what can this portend? If I know my own heart, I shall not allow our relations to be much affected.'

Addison Alexander knew the critical views of German scholars that were being introduced to American audiences, but did not unduly trouble his students with them. His students admired his vast learning, and realized that he was pointing them to the parts of German scholarship that could benefit biblical studies. He had deep respect for the grammatical and philological studies being done on the Continent, and set an example in the way he utilized this work, converting it to productive purposes in the cause of evangelical exegesis. Addison Alexander and his mentor, Charles Hodge, were probably the two American theologians in the mid-nineteenth century who were the most familiar with current German scholarship.

Despite all his personal and academic activity, his own devotions were never neglected. Whatever else could be set aside, they could not. Built into his daily schedule was time to be alone with God and his Word. Quite apart from his preparation for classes, he read and analysed all the Scriptures for his own benefit. The Bible was his grand love, and he had memorized many passages. His eager study of, and zeal for, the Scriptures were apparent to the students, who were conscious of his growth in spiritual things. One of them recorded the remark often made that 'Dr Addison was a man that walked with God, and was evidently growing in grace.' He made no display of his religious life, and was reticent to speak of his personal experiences. On one occasion a rather intense evangelist called to see him and interrogated him as to the evidence of his personal faith. Addison's unwillingness to answer his questions provoked the visitor to say: 'Have you *no* religion, Dr Alexander?' 'None to speak of' was the response.

At the completely opposite end of Addison Alexander's work was his relationship with children, especially the faculty children. He entertained them in his rooms and wrote for them. For several years he put out a handwritten journal, *Wistar's Magazine*, that often contained extremely humorous stories. In one issue he had an account of 'Yes and No', relating to two boys, one of whom could only say 'Yes' while the other could only say 'No'!

The first volume of his commentary on Isaiah was published in 1846. Having seen the second volume of his Isaiah commentary published in 1847, Addison Alexander was free to take up seriously his commentary on the Psalms. His early intention of simply translating Hengstenberg's commentary from German was set aside in favour of a new translation and exegetical treatment. He had come to realize that one of the greatest needs was a literal version of the Hebrew text, and that could not have been achieved by translating an existing translation. It did, however, have that commentary as its basis and he made good use of it, acknowledging his indebtedness to Hengstenberg. This occupied much of his time and energies until it was published in 1850, and it has been republished many times since.

Discussion of various aspects of church order was prevalent in the 1830s and 1840s in the United States. There were two main aspects to this. On the one hand, the Presbyterians were interacting regarding the status of the elder and the role he had to play in the life of the church. While Samuel Miller of Princeton had earlier defended the view that elders should take part in the ordination of ministers, yet by 1840 he was opposing that view and advocating that only ministers should take part in the ordination of ministers. This view was also shared by Charles Hodge. The second main point of controversy was the dispute between Episcopalians on the one hand, and Presbyterians and Congregationalists on the other. Addison Alexander entered the debate by means of a series of articles in the *Biblical Repertory and Princeton Review*. He first discussed the Old and New Testament terms for 'elders' and concluded that the office of elder was the only permanent essential office in the church in either dispensation. As to the role of elders, he argued that elders possessed the highest ministerial powers, including that of discipline and ordination of ministers. The remaining articles defended the Presbyterian position that no apostolical succession, such as defended by Episcopalians, ever existed. These articles were brought together as a book of 180 pages, and published in 1851 under the title, *Essays on the Primitive Church Offices*. It represents one of the best examples we have of his sustained thought and expression on a particular theme.

Amidst all these scholarly activities there are other aspects of Addison Alexander's life that stand in marked contrast. He was always moving from one accommodation to another. As we have mentioned before, he was never content with the position of his books and was constantly moving the shelving. To some extent this desire for change did carry over into his professional life, for at times he would suddenly change the planned work for his classes.

Another form of this need for change was the visits he paid to Philadelphia or New York, staying in favourite hotels and delighting in just watching people and things. Often at meal times he would let the waiters choose from the menu for him. In summer breaks he took longer journeys and even expressed a wish to visit all the main cities in the United States.

6.
Change in direction

Changes were coming at the seminary in the late 1840s, as Archibald Alexander and Samuel Miller were drawing near to the end of their long ministerial and teaching careers. In November 1847 Samuel Miller tendered his resignation to the board of directors, but they refused to accept it. He continued to teach and write, though he was becoming very frail. The last written work he published was a little book entitled *Thoughts on Public Prayer*, which he dedicated 'to the younger ministers, and candidates for the ministry, in the Presbyterian Church in the United States.' He again submitted his resignation in March 1848, and at the age of seventy-nine he was made Emeritus Professor of Ecclesiastical History and Church Government, with his salary to be continued.

Though the two oldest professors, Archibald Alexander and Samuel Miller, were coming near the end of their ministerial careers, yet the faculty, of which they were an important part, was formidable and still very effective. A student gave this summary of it:

> *Dr Archibald Alexander had the keenness of a Kentucky rifle-man in his insight into spiritual experience; Dr Addison Alexander was a whirlwind as a teacher and a preacher; Dr Samuel Miller was a prince in church history and the Chesterfield of the Presbyterian Church; and Dr Charles Hodge was the greatest analytic mind that this country has produced, certainly since the days of Jonathan Edwards.*

Many in the Presbyterian Church thought that Addison Alexander should be moved from the Old Testament to the Church History department. His father, Archibald Alexander, thought that would be a wrong move, as Addison was so gifted in regard to biblical studies that he should be left to teach biblical subjects. The General Assembly, however, at its 1849 meeting, chose his brother, James Waddell Alexander (1804–1859), to succeed Samuel Miller. J. W. Alexander was a gifted pastor and preacher, but he had served on the faculty of Princeton College for eleven years as Professor of Rhetoric and Belles-Lettres. He loved preaching, and for seven years he served as the pastor of the African American Presbyterian Church in Princeton.

The faculty was duly enlarged, but it remained a very unified group of scholars who knew one another well and who held to the same doctrinal convictions. Archibald Alexander was working alongside two of his sons, James and Addison, his old colleague Samuel Miller continued some teaching, and Charles Hodge completed the faculty. Miller's contribution to the life of the seminary did not last for much longer, for by the end of 1849 his health had declined markedly. His new colleague, J. W. Alexander, visited him for the last time on 31 December 1849, when he knelt and prayed with him. Samuel Miller passed away on 7 January 1850, bringing to an end a teaching career at Princeton of thirty-seven years. The funeral sermon was preached by Dr Archibald Alexander, who in the course of his address said of his old friend: 'I have never known a man more entirely free from vain glory, envy, and jealousy.'

This close-knit group of teachers, already broken by Miller's death, was not to remain together for long, for in 1851 J. W. Alexander, missing the pastoral ministry, accepted a call from Fifth Avenue Presbyterian Church in New York. As his successor, the General Assembly chose his brother, Addison Alexander. It was with reluctance that he accepted this decision, and soon was immersed in the study of church history.

In changing subject areas Addison Alexander did not leave behind all the characteristics he had displayed earlier when teaching Hebrew and Old Testament. Just as he often altered course mid-stream then, so now with his teaching of church history. He lectured without notes, but had all the facts and figures at his finger tips. Some of his students thought he was too fickle. Although teaching church history was not his own choice, he became reconciled to the decision and set about his task. By mid-1852 he commented in a letter to his brother James that he was at ease as to his professorship, and that he was quite willing to remain in his present position.

He had not lost his love of languages, and returned with vigour to pursuing Sanscrit and Turkish. He also turned back to all his old 'irons in the fire', as he described them — the Septuagint, the Aramaic targums, the Latin Vulgate, the classics, and even chemistry! He was also reading up on Danish and French history, and included the book by the Scottish self-taught geologist, Hugh Miller, entitled *The Old Red Sandstone.*

This period of his life was marked by the death of his father, Dr Archibald Alexander. His brother James had been on a trip to Europe and only returned to Princeton on 16 October 1851. His father was very weak, and though he walked downstairs to his study on the following day, he had to be carried back up to his bedroom where he died on 22 October. His mind was clear to the end, and he spoke of his undoubted confidence of his acceptance with God through the Redeemer.

The funeral took place two days later, with Dr John McDowell, the oldest director of the seminary, preaching on Revelation 14:13: 'And I heard a voice from heaven saying unto me, Write, Blessed are the dead which die in the Lord from henceforth: Yea, saith the Spirit, that they may rest from their labours: and their works do follow them.' Three synods of the church were meeting nearby, so members were able to be present. The Presbytery of New Brunswick acted as pall-bearers, and so many were present that some ministers were even sitting on the floor of the church. While an observer said that the light of the resurrection and of immortality dispelled the shadows of death, yet Addison Alexander was deeply stirred by his father's death. He sat motionless until, during the singing of a hymn, he was so emotionally upset that his sobbing could be heard by all. Then he controlled himself, and was again calm and motionless.

With his father's death, Addison assumed the role of head of the house. He moved back into the same room on the ground floor in the north-west corner of the family home on the campus that he had occupied ten years previously. In addition to his mother, two of his brothers were still living there, William and Archibald, and his sister, Janetta. On one occasion as his mother was house cleaning, she announced she would clean and arrange his study. He agreed, and she went ahead but took a note of everything and replaced them in the exact position she had found them. She thought Addison would be very pleased with what she had done, but when he returned and went into his study he said in a very disappointed voice, 'Why, you have everything just as it was!' His nephew and biographer, Henry Carrington Alexander, in referring to his constant desire for change and variation, had a term for it. He called it his love of 'local novelty'.

As a pastime he liked to look out from his study window and watch all those passing by. He knew all about the pedestrians, as he did about the carriages and carts that came along. But this was not his main activity, which remained his books and his study. When one of his brothers was away for a couple of months, he missed him so much that he took up two languages. One was Danish, which he took up again with enthusiasm, and after reading the four Gospels, Acts and Revelation, he took up a history of Denmark in Danish, and to his own surprise found that he could read it 'very fluently with a dictionary'.

He assiduously cared for his mother, taking her the following summer on a visit to New York and New England. Wherever she wanted to go, he took her. Whatever she wanted to have, he tried to provide it. She did not outlive her husband for long, but passed away on 6 October 1852, with several of the family members present and another of her sons kneeling in prayer by the bed.

His mind was constantly occupied with consideration of what subject on which to work and publish. To his brother James, in a letter of March 1853, he confided: 'I am suffering for want of a book to write, being paralysed by infirmity of choice. I am not at all ambitious in the matter, being only anxious to discover how my gifts and materials could be employed most usefully.'

Addison decided that he would, after an absence of twenty years, return to Europe, and in the summer of 1853 he took with him Dr Charles Hodge's son, Caspar Wistar Hodge (1830–1891). He was twenty-two years of age, and was Addison's student and friend. When he was about twelve years of age, Addison suggested that he tutor him before he entered Princeton College. For two years this relationship continued, and when Caspar Wistar did enrol at Princeton College, he was extremely well prepared, and graduated in 1848 at the top of his class. For most of the trip to Europe they were together, though on some occasions they separated and did different things. They sailed from New York on 18 May 1853, and arrived at Liverpool on Sunday 29 May. It was a busy summer — two days in Liverpool, seven days in Edinburgh, two days in Melrose and Abbotsford, six days in London, six days in Oxford and Cambridge, and seventeen in Paris. From Paris they did a circuit visiting Nancy, Basel, Heidelberg, Mannheim, Cologne, Arnhem, Utrecht, Amsterdam, Rotterdam, Harlem, Leiden, the Hague, Antwerp, Ghent, Bruges and Ostend. Back in England they spent a further week in London before taking a quick trip to Dublin, then across to Manchester, and finally reached Liverpool, from where they sailed on 20 August for New York.

During the trip Addison kept a very full diary with detailed notes on the religious services he attended. He went to hear Dr McNeile in St Paul's Church, Liverpool, but felt there was no power in his preaching and recorded that he would not cross the street to hear him again! How different it was in Edinburgh! Dr Thomas Guthrie (1803–73) was not preaching in his church, Free St John's, but rather Dr Thomas Chalmers' (1780–1847) son-in-law, Dr William Hanna (1808–82), was occupying the pulpit at both services. So the visitors went down to the west end of Princes Street and listened to Dr Robert Candlish at Free St George's. Addison gave a detailed account of the service, including a description of the interior of the church, the singing, and, of course, the preaching. The text was 2 Corinthians 11:3: 'But I fear, lest by any means, as the serpent beguiled Eve through his subtilty, so your minds should be corrupted from the simplicity that is in Christ.' The picture he painted of Candlish was to compare him 'to that of a sickly boy, just roused from sleep, and without any washing or combing — his eyes scarcely open and his hair disordered — forced into the ugliest and clumsiest black gown you can imagine, dragged into the pulpit and compelled to preach.' Though Candlish read from a manuscript, scarcely looking up at the congregation, Addison was captivated by the sermon, and went back in the evening to hear him complete his exposition of the text. The climax of the sermon, he wrote, 'was certainly one of the grandest bursts of eloquence that I have ever heard. If Chalmers was as much above this man in actual power as he is in frame, he was almost superhuman.'

Clearly Addison had made a list of preachers whom he wished to hear. In London he listened to Dr James Hamilton (1814–67). In Paris he listened to Dr Adolphe Monod (1802–56) preaching on Psalm 20:3: 'Remember all thy offerings and accept thy burnt sacrifices.' The next week he went to the Salle Taitbout and heard M. Pressensé on 1 John 1:8, dealing with the various ways that men will deny that they are sinners before God. The most impressive part of the sermon was when the preacher pictured God bringing a man to the foot of the cross, and to all the teaching about the gospel the unconverted sinner's answer was, '*Mensonge! Mensonge! Mensonge!*' [A lie! A lie! A lie!].

In typical fashion Addison Alexander commented in his diary on many incidents during the trip, including the cruise by steamer on the Rhine. He was always attracted by people, and described the behaviour of two Englishmen who would approach other passengers and speak to them in English. Quite frequently they happened to approach people who could only reply in broken English. He was also attracted by two Roman Catholic clergy, one a German abbot and the other an elderly French priest. He heard them speaking Latin as it was their only common language. He had often wished to hear a conversation in Latin and so, as he sat at a nearby table, he followed their conversation. A Scots or Irish clergyman accompanied by a young student was attracted for the same reason, as were Bonn students who stood close by, listening to the Latin conversation and laughing among themselves about it.

He also visited the Netherlands, and found the people more like the Americans than any he had seen in Europe. The language, in its tone and accent, was more like English than any European language he had heard. His comment on it was: 'Its intonations are as much like ours as the Scotch or Irish. It is also very musical, so that when you hear it close at hand, it sounds like German spoken by an Englishman, with a suppression of the harsh sounds.'

In settling back into his Princeton work after his second European tour, many aspects of Addison's life did not change. He was still the avid reader, even following the example of his brother James in having a book open when he was shaving! He remained the student of languages and, above all, of the Bible. Being Professor of Church History did not mean that he was cut off from biblical studies, for part of his course work was Old Testament history and the early history of the Christian church.

While teaching many different subjects, Addison Alexander continued to work on commentaries. The plan was for himself, his brother James and Charles Hodge to produce a set of commentaries on the whole of the New Testament. He himself was to write on the Gospels and Acts, his brother James on the Pastoral Epistles, and Charles Hodge the remaining books. The original vision was never accomplished, but Addison published on Acts (1857), Mark

(1858), and he had completed his commentary on the first sixteen chapters of Matthew at the time of his death, and it was published posthumously by Charles Scribner in New York in 1861. Hodge completed commentaries on Ephesians (1856), 1 Corinthians (1857) and 2 Corinthians (1859). He had published on Romans much earlier (1835), with an abridged version appearing the following year, and it was reprinted in England in 1838. Adophe Monod translated the 1836 edition into French, and it was published in 1839.

His diary remained very similar to earlier years. Here is an example from early 1854:

> *Feb. 2 Lectured to the third Class on the chronology of the Gospels. Continued Eadie on Ephesians, Caspari's Arabic Grammar, Keil's Einleitung ins Alte Test [Introduction to the Old Testament], the Koran in Arabic with Kasimirski's version, Canticles [Song of Solomon] in Greek, and Mark in Syriac. Finished the second book of Xenophon's Hellenica. Read Lord Brougham's admirable speech on the Reform Bill (1831). Began a list of the grammatical forms actually used in the Greek Testament.*

Amidst so many demands on his time Addison Alexander still found time for considerable correspondence. Like his colleagues, he had watched the career of Dr Philip Schaff (1819–1893), the Swiss theologian and historian who taught at the small seminary of the German Reformed Church at Mercersburg, Pennsylvania, and later at Union Theological Seminary, New York. He and his brother James were more appreciative of Schaff than Charles Hodge. It is clear that Schaff reciprocated the feelings for, from a letter of

Addison Alexander to Schaff in 1854, we know that Schaff had approached him to cooperate in the preparation of a book on church history. Alexander, in the midst of his own writing, replied to Schaff that he could not see his way clear 'to engage in any joint task of the kind you mention.'

In the mid 1850s he was working on his commentary on Acts, though he vacillated at times whether it would be better to have a series of essays on Acts or a commentary on it comparable to his one on the Psalms. He had actually started on a more detailed commentary comparable to his one on Isaiah, but when 100 pages had been set up, he changed his mind. His publisher, Mr Scribner of New York, must have been very tolerant to accommodate all the changes in plans. Charles Hodge remarked that 'his impatience of sameness was a great inconvenience to him. He would often begin to write on some subject and get tired of it and throw it aside.' What he needed, as he acknowledged, was for the publisher to start to print and he then felt locked-in to a method, and he had to keep ahead of the printer.

When his commentary on Acts was published in October 1856, he used it in his classes. His nephew Henry was a student at the seminary at that time, and he said that Addison gave a very illuminating commentary on his own book.

At this time there was quite a spiritual movement in the college. The request was made that Dr Addison Alexander should preach in the college chapel, having not done so for some years. This he declined, suggesting that Dr Hodge was a better choice, particularly as his spiritual experience had started when he was a college student. Addison Alexander felt that in the circumstances Dr Hodge could understand the students better and could, therefore, exert a stronger influence on them. However, Professor Cameron, in pressing the request, said to him, 'Doctor, excuse me if I say I think *you underrate your influence with our students*.' This seemed to sway his mind and, putting off another engagement, he preached in the chapel on the text, 'Come, for all things are now ready' (Luke 14:17). One minister later testified that he was converted under that sermon. Addison often felt the barrenness of his ministry, but this was not just an isolated case of spiritual fruit from his ministry. This sermon was later included in his posthumous volumes of sermons (vol. 1, pp. 209-26).

In 1856 Addison's brother Samuel was installed as pastor of Fifteenth Street Presbyterian Church in the city of New York, with his brother James preaching on that occasion. This induction took place just before the meetings of the General Assemblies of both the Old School and the New School. Both James and Addison commented on things at the Old School Assembly, with Addison delighted with the sermon of Dr J. H. Thornwell (1812–1862) on foreign missions. He also sat in and listened to some of the debates in the New School Assembly. Dr Robert L. Dabney accompanied him back to Princeton and spent a day with him. They talked over matters in relation to their work in seminaries and within the wider church. Dabney was impressed with Addison Alexander who, though having severe toothache, continued to care for him and carried on conversation. 'I ascertained,' Dabney wrote afterwards, 'that he was a man who thought for himself, and had original views, many of them far from harmonious with prevalent and fashionable ecclesiasticism.'

He did not always venture north to New York or New England on his vacation tours, but on rarer occasions he went south. On one such trip he stayed in Richmond, Virginia, with Dr T. V. Moore (1818–71), one of his own former students, who, in the introduction to his commentary on Haggai, Zechariah and Malachi published in 1856, referred to 'the rare privilege' he had had of listening to the lectures of Addison Alexander. While Addison was with the Moore family, he fell in with the normal arrangements in the household, and entertained the children by inventing plays and telling them stories. He even taught them a simple alphabet that they could use for secret correspondence! Once he was missing, and they found him in the room next to his with one of the children who was sick and whom he was entertaining with stories. Looking back on the visit, Moore remarked that he had noticed in Addison small symptoms of diabetes, that he didn't think of at the time, but later realized that they were symptoms of an illness that resulted in his premature death.

From Richmond he crossed the mountains to Lexington and Staunton. While at Lexington he met Dr Robert Dabney (1820–98) of Union Theological Seminary, Virginia, and they spent two days together in the same house. Dabney heard him preach twice and enjoyed conversation with him. While noting that he was unobtrusive and retiring, yet Dabney found that Alexander responded positively so that they had good interaction with one another. People in Virginia weren't accustomed to hearing sermons read, but though Addison used a very crumpled manuscript, the people were delighted and profited from his preaching. Once he was called on unexpectedly to preach on this visit, and he spoke as fluently as if he had a full manuscript with him.

By the end of January 1858, Addison was working on the third chapter of Matthew. In writing to his brother James he noted that he was making progress with Matthew: 'The reading is delightful: the writing less so.' For a time he gave up work on the commentary, for he recalled that his father had said that one should never prosecute a work unless it was *con amore* [with love]. The onset of diabetes may well have played a part in this intermission from writing, but soon he picked it up again. Up till May he continued his usual routine of lectures, and then was away from Princeton for over two months. First he went south by steamer to Virginia, and there met up with his sister Jane, who travelled back to Princeton with him. Almost immediately he went via Philadelphia and Baltimore to New York, where he was busy correcting the proofs of his commentary on Mark. He had to write the introduction to his commentary, and this only took him three days (21–23 July). On 16 August he left for a visit to Canada, returning to Princeton on 30 August.

Some of his most endearing characteristics came out in this period of his life. He sent gifts of money or books to relatives. An acquaintance was given a trunk full of books to read, along with the offer of his whole library! He kept what he called his 'Two-Penny Book' in which he recorded the names of visitors to the family home, and any matters of interest concerning them. His interest in children was as strong as ever. For a needy student, he made financial provision so that he could continue his studies.

Addison Alexander's friendship with his student and then colleague, William Henry Green, was very strong. He made available to him much of his own research into Hebrew grammar and philology, and clearly encouraged him to go to Germany to study under E. W. Hengstenberg. The influence of Alexander on Green can be traced down through his life. After almost fifty years of teaching at Princeton, Green wrote a large volume entitled *The Unity of the Book of Genesis*. He argued that the literary unity of the book points to unity of authorship, and the influence of Alexander is apparent in the way he developed his argument. Late in the book he quotes from one of his unpublished lectures, a scholar whom he calls 'my distinguished predecessor' (p. 565, n. 1). When Green published his *General Introduction to the Old Testament: The Canon* in 1899, he included as the first five pages a lecture by Addison Alexander. This was his explanation for its insertion:

> *This brief sketch is extracted from an unpublished lecture of my former friend, preceptor, and colleague,* Dr Joseph *Addison Alexander, for many years the ornament and pride of Princeton Theological Seminary. It was written in 1843, and is here inserted as a memento of a brilliant scholar and in humble acknowledgement of indebtedness to his instructions.*

It may not have been a wise choice to include a discussion so dated as that in his book, but Green wished to place on record his relationship with his mentor and point to the continuity of approach between Alexander and himself. Issues changed over the course of his career, and he forged new pathways of study for himself, but he never forgot his teacher and friend.

7.

The final years

While William Henry Green was on a trip to Europe in 1858, Addison Alexander again taught Hebrew. He did so with the same enthusiasm for it that he had shown in his early years on the faculty. His colleague Alexander McGill wrote: 'The whole term of his employment was one of exhilaration to him; like that of a child recovering possession of a toy which he had been tired of once, and now recognized in all its original attractions.' As far back as 1854 Addison had expressed the conviction that in teaching church history he was in the wrong department, which contradicted what he had said in 1852. While one of his later successors in teaching church history thought that he was absolutely fitted for this subject, some of his students at the time would have disagreed. He changed his methods, as he had done earlier in regard to teaching the Old Testament, and students complained he was 'so fickle'. He had conversations with his brother James in 1854, who in his diary recorded this: 'Letters from Addison. I lament his discontent in his present situation.'

It had become clear to him that he was far better suited for exposition of the Bible, and areas such as archaeology and philology rather than church history. Accordingly, he made the proposal early in 1859 that his colleague, Dr McGill, take over the church history teaching, in addition to his work with regard to church government. While he thought that Dr McGill's workload would increase if this was done, yet he believed he himself would be better suited teaching New Testament. The trustees of the seminary and the General Assembly agreed, and so Addison Alexander was transferred to the chair of Hellenistic and New Testament Literature. There was no doubt that he was equipped to teach in this area, and the Greek language had become one of his favourite subject areas many years previously. To his brother James he wrote:

> *Thus I began my course [of teaching at the seminary] with a divided heart, and though I never disliked teaching Hebrew, but preferred it much to all my other Seminary duties, I still spent much time upon Greek in private; not without a secret feeling of unfaithfulness to my official obligations.*

His brother James had been encouraging him for some time to transfer back to a biblical area of instruction rather than church history. Addison was glad that James had lived long enough to see this change take effect.

In assessing his own ministry he seemed increasingly fearful that his life would prove to be worthless. He longed to preach with greater simplicity, just as Paul, or Luther, or Calvin did. This was expressed in his journal:

> *As life runs on, I feel the seriousness of my situation as a minister, but oh, how little improvement! Oh, my ascended Lord and Master! Be pleased to anoint me afresh for my ministry, send me some new and special grace, and cast me not aside as a useless instrument: for Christ's sake. Amen.*

The passing of the years had not changed Addison Alexander's love of travel. In the early summer of 1859 he took what he called 'a great circle,' travelling from New York up into Canada and back to New York. He went through Boston, Portland, Quebec, Montreal, Toronto, Buffalo, Detroit, Chicago, Springfield, St Louis, Vincennes, Cincinnati, Columbus, Pittsburg, Harrisburg, Easton, Somerville and Elizabethport. In describing this trip in a letter to his brother James, he claimed that he was as perfectly at home in the streets of Chicago, St Louis, Cincinnati and Pittsburg, as those of Philadelphia or New York. His colleague, A. T. McGill, in writing about his love of change and variety, wrote: 'Nothing but old doctrines and old friends could he adhere to with immutable interest and fondness.'

But Addison Alexander's life was drawing to a close. His brother James died in July 1859 in Virginia, where he had gone on a visit as he recuperated from a serious illness. James was a pastor at heart, and never happier than when he was fulfilling various roles in the life of his congregation: 'I miss my old women; and especially my weekly catechumens, my sick rooms, my rapid walks, and my nights of downright fatigue,' as he had written in October 1849. James was buried beside his parents in the old cemetery in Princeton, while at the memorial service in his church in New York, Charles Hodge took Acts 9:20 as his text: 'He preached Christ.'

James and Addison were so close to one another that James' death was an immense blow to his brother. Addison's health was already an issue, especially due to the fact that he had developed diabetes. An added problem was that he was not at all careful about his health. Charles Hodge, in reflecting on Addison Alexander's character and work, pointed out how there were certain subjects, especially in the area of philosophy, that he did not want to read or talk about. Then Hodge added these words:

> *It was especially such subjects as anatomy, physiology, hygiene, of which he determined he would know nothing. He had seen how superficial knowledge on this matter had rendered men hypochondriac, and consequently miserable and burdensome. He therefore went to the opposite extreme, and was really so ignorant that he did not know how to take care of himself. That is, he would unconsciously violate the laws of health, especially by exposure, greatly to his own injury.*

As already mentioned, Addison's health was already an issue before James died, but his depression because of it was now an added factor. He lost weight, and appeared drawn and haggard. At first, all he complained about was extreme dryness of the throat, but then tiredness, a rasping cough, and problems with his breathing. His students were starting to notice and talk about his loss of weight and the pale colour of his face. He carried on his class work with great difficulty, before he had to cease due to increasing weakness. However, in the last few months of his life he still persisted with his vast reading schedule, including material in Hebrew, Aramaic, German, French, Greek, Danish and Italian. These are the final entries in his journal:

Friday, Jan. 20 [1860] — Read over my analysis of Matthew xvii-xxviii. Reading as usual. Letter from John Hall, declining to come, except in case of urgent need. Wrote to Moffat, requesting him to preach for me, which he agreed to do.

Saturday, Jan. 21 — Finished the second volume of Steven's History of Methodism, *begun Jan. 3d. Visit from W. H. G[reen]. Wrote to Dr. J. H. Jones.*

Lord's Day, Jan. 22 — Nehemiah in Coverdale; Hodge on 2d Corinthians; Schultz on Deuteronomy; Morning Service and Litany; Episcopal Psalms and Hymns; three of my brother's 'Discourses on Common Topics of Faith and Practice'; ten of Adolph Monod's Dying Speeches *(or* Adieux à ses amis et à l'église*); Anderson's* Colonial Church History; The Presbyterian; *finished Ecclesiastes in Hebrew, with the Chaldee Paraphrase (begun Dec. 28).*

Monday, Jan. 23 — Finished (in bed) Coverdale's Version of Nehemiah (begun Jan. 11). Visits from Dr Atwater and Moffat, the latter of whom preached for me in the chapel yesterday. Finished Dicken's Tale of Two Cities, *a powerful tragic fiction, unrelieved by any comic element; for Cruncher is a miserable failure. Other reading as usual.*

Tuesday, Jan. 24 — Left the house for the first time since my memorable return on the 28th of November [from Philadelphia]. Took a drive with my sister in Dr Hodge's carriage.

Wednesday, Jan. 25 — Shaved by Gilbert Scudder. S. D. A. [his brother, Samuel Davies Alexander] from New York and back. Reading as usual.

During the last weeks of his life family and friends visited him, but even when one of them commented on his weakness, he did not seem to understand just how weak he was. He had committed some more hymns to memory including Charlotte Elliott's 'Just as I am without one plea, save that thy blood was shed for me', Charles Wesley's hymn beginning with 'Come, let us anew our journey pursue', and Watts' 'Show pity, Lord, O Lord, forgive; let a repenting rebel live', and they were a comfort to him. He was only confined to bed for one day, and that bed was brought down into his study. He passed into the presence of the Lord on Saturday afternoon, 28 January 1860.

The following day the usual Sunday conference took place at the seminary. The topic chosen the previous week was 'The Lord reigneth'. Charles Hodge could not control his emotion, and was unable to read the usual chapter. When the time came for remarks, he said, 'We were assembled as a bereaved family, and would spend the time that we were together in talking of him whom we loved and who had been taken from us. How premature his death appears to human view and how irreparable his loss!'

The funeral took place on Tuesday 31 January in First Presbyterian Church, Princeton, with Dr Hall of Trenton preaching. He was buried in the old Princeton cemetery just near the grave of Jonathan Edwards.

It was not only at Princeton or within the church community that there was deep lamentation at the sudden and early passing of Addison Alexander. He was a member of the American Philosophical Association. This was a society founded by Benjamin Franklin (1706–1790), though it fell on some hard times a little later. By the mid nineteenth century, it was flourishing. Knowing his dislike of philosophy, it may seem strange that he was a member of this society. However, it must be remembered that the society was dealing with scientific subjects as well as strictly philosophical topics, and this would have been well within Addison Alexander's range of interest. In this society an obituary notice was presented by Dr John Leyburn (1814–1893), minister of Petersburg Presbyterian Church, Virginia. Leyburn had studied at Princeton College during Addison Alexander's time, and he reviewed his achievements, including his command of language that, Leyburn said, 'has seldom been surpassed. He always seemed to have at his tongue's end the most appropriate words to express his ideas, and it was a pleasure to sit and listen even to the cadence and flow of his copious vocabulary.' In concluding the obituary, Leyburn said,

> *His splendid intellect and his vast resources were all brought into subjection to his Christian faith. He had no fellowship with that pride of learning which exalts itself even above the revelations of Divine wisdom. He was as lowly in his estimation of himself, as he was exalted in the opinions of his fellow-men, and especially did he regard himself as incompetent to sit in judgment upon his Maker, and decide, as too many attempt to do, what he should and what he should not have revealed.*

8.
Writing ministry

From the time that Addison Alexander began teaching at Princeton Seminary his most enduring legacy is in his exegetical work. Some of it is only known because students left detailed notes of the work he did with them, while his major contributions were his commentaries on Isaiah and the Psalms of the Old Testament, and Mark and Acts of the New Testament. He was pre-eminently an exegete of Scripture, and it was this characteristic that left its mark on his students, and ensured continued publication and use of his commentaries. He was the American Hengstenberg, writing with much of the same breadth of knowledge of contemporary scholarship but staking out his own evangelical convictions.

The earliest attempt he made was on the book of Leviticus. He had a small class of private students, but clearly he prepared extremely well for it. This course he first offered in 1837 and also in the following year, and at some later stages he also taught on this book. While he concentrated on the early chapters, some students revealed how he had ventured beyond mere exegesis to discuss matters such as how the ceremonial sacrificial system and the tabernacle were significant as part of God's revelation of himself.

Two other biblical books he dealt with were Nahum and Hosea, the first lectures dating from 1838 and the second from 1842. Extant students' notes show how meticulous he was in preparation for the classes, and how systematically he treated the text. As in his other exegetical writings, he was intent on showing the meaning of the Hebrew text as he set it in its historical context. Like his mentor Hengstenberg, he drew upon secondary sources but used them with discretion. He was very familiar with a wide range of scholarship, both Jewish and Christian.

As already noted, he began to write on the book of Isaiah from an early period. He first taught on Isaiah in 1834, and his interest was so aroused that in the following year he started collecting material with a view to publication. In 1836 he began writing his commentary, but the first volume of it was not published until 1846.

His aim was quite plain. He intended to write a commentary that would benefit preachers so that they would be provided with 'a partial succedaneum [substitute] for the many costly books' and also to let them 'profit by the latest philological improvements and discoveries.'

His method of working was interesting, as his youngest brother, Henry Alexander, recorded:

> *When he was writing his commentary on Isaiah, he caused to be made two standing desks reaching from one end of the room to the other in his large study. These were two stories high ... I should estimate that these stands held about fifty volumes, all of them open. He would first pass down the line where the commentaries were, then go to the lexicons, then to other books; and when he was through, he would hurry to the table at which he wrote, write rapidly for a few minutes, and then return again to the books: and this he would repeat again and again, for ten or twelve hours together.*

His brother also added an amusing note: 'He was much troubled with toothache and the hot weather affected him a good deal, and I have often heard him say that the best relief from both of these annoyances was some difficult passage to explain.'

In his diary he noted the progress he was making, and continued to comment on his procedure. He temporarily set aside his work on Isaiah in 1842, having become overwhelmed with the task, and worked on a commentary on Obadiah. However, he soon resumed work on Isaiah. Here is a sample from his diary that gives some idea of his continuing method. On 2 November 1843, he wrote:

> *Read Jarchi, Kimchi, Aben-Ezra, the Michlal Jophi, Luther, Calvin, Grotius, Junius, Cocceius, the* Dutch Annotations, Pool's Synopsis, *Vitringa, Clericus, Gill, J. H. Michaelis, J. D. Michaelis, Lowth, Rosenmüller, Augusti, Gesenius, Maurer, Hitzig, Hendewerk, Barnes, Henderson, De Wette, and Umbreit, on Isaiah x. 33, 34. Wrote the first draft of a commentary on these verses.*

By 1846 he had completed the first volume, and it was published. The second volume of *The Latter Prophecies of Isaiah* was published the following year. Dr John Eadie (1810–1876) of Scotland edited the two volumes four years after Alexander's death, and they were published in 1865. The combined volumes were preceded by a lengthy introduction amounting to seventy-eight pages in the Scottish edition. One factor that stands out about the introduction is the wide range of scholarly opinion of which Alexander makes mention. In addition to many of the medieval Jewish scholars, he refers to over fifty scholars, the majority of whom were Continental, mainly German but also including Dutch. The few English writers of whom he made mention include Gill, Lowth, Barnes and Henderson.

The first part of the introduction was a discussion of the Greek and Hebrew terms for 'prophet'. He took the position that the primary import of the biblical terms was not denoting foresight or prediction of the future. The main significance of the Hebrew word, he contended, 'signify specifically one who speaks (or the act of speaking) for God, not only in his name and by his authority, but under his influence, in other words, by divine inspiration'. The precise meaning of the Hebrew word 'prophet' (*nâvî'*) was made plain by its use in Exodus 7:1: 'See, I made you a god to Pharaoh, and Aaron your brother shall be your prophet.'

After considering the meaning of the name 'Isaiah' ('salvation is of Jehovah') and a brief survey of his life and times, Alexander referred to the use of the book of Isaiah in the New Testament. Going by the present chapter division, forty-eight of the chapters are either directly quoted or alluded to by the New Testament writers, while all the evidence points to 'the book of the prophet Isaiah' (Luke 4:17) used by Jesus and his apostles being the same as the one in current Bibles. Until the middle of the eighteenth century no one, whether Jewish or Christian, had doubted the authenticity of the book.

That discussion paved the way for treatment of the question of the unity of the book, specifically of chapters 1–39. He lists some of the divergent views of many of the Dutch and German writers, and then attempts to point out the difficulties in holding to their positions. Some passages, such as chapter 21, were regarded by various scholars as a *vaticinium ex eventu* (a prophecy after the event).

Those prophets, Alexander believed, were not part of a long line of prophets with unbroken continuity who automatically succeeded to office. Rather, they were individually called by God and fitted for his service as part of the fulfilment of the promise of Deuteronomy 18. The usual manner in which they received revelation was by vision, just as Micaiah *saw* Israel scattered on the hills like sheep without a shepherd (1 Kings 22:17), or Isaiah *saw* the Lord sitting on a throne (Isa. 6:1).

Chapters 40–66 were also discussed extensively. First of all, Alexander referred to the prophet's role in correcting false ideas within Israel/Judah regarding the place of the Mosaic ceremonial system and the exclusion of Gentiles from God's kingdom. While some regarded the ceremonies as a pretext for introducing idolatrous practices, others thought that the sacrifices were truly efficacious. In contending against these errors the prophets, who had up to this point spoken against them, now had the Lord's instruction to write their messages as a written record that testified against such perversions.

The unity of the book of Isaiah was dealt with at some length by Alexander. He began by arguing against the two common arguments in favour of an author for chapters 40–66 other than Isaiah of Jerusalem. These were the supposed allusions to exile in Babylon, and the language and style that were not those of Isaiah or Jerusalem. The whole book, he believed, was one continuous discourse, in which the prophet came back time and again to the same themes, though modifying them in form and the way in which the arguments were marshalled. Alexander presented eleven arguments against the denial of Isaianic authorship of chapters 40–66, including the uniform testimony of the Jews. The references to Jerusalem and Judah show that the writer was describing features of his homeland, while the characterization of the exile is clear enough, yet not necessarily the work of a contemporary writer.

The last part of the introduction to chapters 40–66 is a survey of their interpretation, with reference to early church fathers through to commentators in Alexander's own day. Many of these presentations were set aside since they were prompted by a desire to prove that the writer must have been contemporary with the exile. Close familiarity with the Dutch and German writers is very apparent. As for Alexander himself, he set out the five main themes that are developed in Isaiah.

1. The carnal Israel, the Jewish nation of Israel, in its proud self-reliance;
2. The spiritual Israel, the true church, viewed as the object of God's favour;
3. The exile in Babylon and the restoration as the most important time-slot between the date of the prediction and the coming of the Messiah;
4. The advent itself, with depiction of the character of the Saviour;
5. The character of the Church as a whole.

The edition by Eadie was important as it introduced Alexander's work to British readers. Not all the reviews were complimentary. While recognizing the vast scholarship displayed in it, some felt that it contained too much concerning the views of others and too little of Alexander's own position. One Scottish reviewer said this about it:

> *Well, there was such an excess of detail in the statement of other people's opinions on every passage of the least importance — indeed, on almost every verse, not to say clause and word — and such a deficiency in the statement of his own, that one had to hunt up and down through a paragraph or two, to discover the author's own view of a passage, nor in some cases could he be quite sure that he had got it even then.*

This criticism is correct, and a similar opinion was voiced in America. It was felt that the commentary was too learned. Stemming from his method of consulting so many writers on a passage, the commentary was overloaded with references to the views of other scholars. This may have been the deference of a young scholar (bearing in mind that he was only thirty-seven years of age when he published his first volume on Isaiah), and a criticism that could not be levelled as much against his later commentaries, both on Old Testament as well as New Testament books. It is also true that in referring to so many Continental critical discussions, he inadvertently disseminated their views to American readers.

Some criticisms probably did not surprise Dr John Eadie, for in his preface he wrote that he did not 'mean to make this republished Exposition the theme of unqualified or indiscriminate eulogy'. He knew that not every reader was going to assent to all the hypotheses he put forward or 'be converted to his marked and favourite interpretations of those paragraphs and sections, the precise meaning and fulfilment of which are in the present day topics of keen and protracted controversy'. He knew, though, that the republication in Britain of the volumes on Isaiah were going to be 'cordially welcomed and speedily naturalised among us'.

Alexander had noted numerous corrections and improvements to his commentary as he started work on a revised edition. He was not spared to see that appear, but Dr Eadie was given the marked copy by a friend and incorporated the notes in the edition he published.

This combined volume on Isaiah was influential from the time it was published. E. J. Young (1907–1968), in his large three-volumed commentary on Isaiah, refers to it as 'exemplary'. He adds: 'It is absolutely true to the Scriptures, rich in insight and in discussion of the Hebrew forms, and filled with valuable comment.' He refers to Alexander's discussions over 120 times, almost as many as his references to Calvin. In his *Studies in Isaiah*, Young points to characteristics of Alexander beyond his grammatical and philological knowledge. He wrote that Alexander had 'certain other qualifications which are indispensable for one who would expound the Scriptures. He had ... a sincere and humble piety coupled with firm faith in the Bible and reverence for the Bible as the Word of God.' John D. W. Watts, in his commentary on Isaiah in the Word series (1994), lists it as one of the excellent conservative commentaries that appeared in the middle of the nineteenth century. It is still listed as part of a select bibliography in many modern commentaries, a testimony to its enduring usefulness.

Shortly before these volumes on Isaiah were in print, Alexander turned back again to work on the book of Psalms. He had prepared lectures on the Psalms from January 1838, and his diary shows how intense was his preparation. In extant student notes from 1839 he summarized his longer discussion on method. His 'Directions for reading a passage' involved three steps:

> *1st. Read the E[nglish] version to see what is obscure, and mark such obscurities. 2d. Read grammatically having these difficulties particularly in view. 3d. Read over the whole, find what is the general subject, what is the scope of the whole, and what its bearing [is], if it has any, upon the New Testament.*

These rules have to be set alongside Alexander's note regarding things that were to be avoided in biblical exegesis:

1. Confusing the idea of familiarity with the text with a thorough understanding of it — one of the evils of long acquaintance with the Scriptures. Allied to this is a losing sight of the changes of meaning of old English words in the translation, e.g. quick (alive) — hell (place of departed spirits) — prevent (come before) — carriages (baggage);
2. Considering the verses as separate aphorisms, without attention to the context and whole scope — an evil of the division into verses;
3. Neglecting the connection and mutual bearing of the Old and New Testaments;
4. Not uniting a critical and practical reading of the Scripture; not making exegesis subservient to devotion;
5. Not making exegesis practical as to sermonizing ... having but a limited round of texts. The opposite however [is] to be avoided, i.e. the selection of quaint, out of the way and fantastical texts.

The notes of students show that in classroom teaching he dealt with the problematic words and phrases in a passage, and also with the most interesting aspects. He was not afraid to point out the inadequacies of the Authorized Version. Then he moved on to the views of ancient and contemporary writers on the passage, before setting out his interpretation of the word or passage in question.

Early in 1849 he wrote to his brother James about his commentary on the Psalms. He had had correspondence with the prospective publisher (Baker & Scribner of New

York) about the typeface, the paper and the size, but he was content to let his brother make the final decisions on these matters for him. The letter goes on to describe his aim for this commentary:

> *My plan is to convey to the English reader, in the shortest space, the true sense, as determined by the best and latest exegesis. This I do, when it is possible, by mere translation; if not, by paraphrase; if more is wanted, by brief comment. If I merely brought the substance and results of Hengstenberg's book within the English reader's reach, I should think it an invaluable gift. After much thought I have again resolved to leave the 'practique part' to other hands. I would rather do one thing well than two things badly.*

The introduction to *The Psalms: Translated and Explained* is nowhere near as extensive as the one for Isaiah, being only about seven pages in length. It is important, though, as it spells out something about his method. He was aiming particularly at the needs of ministers whom, he says, 'are better able than himself to erect a doctrinal, devotional, or practical superstructure on the exegetical basis which he has endeavoured here to furnish.' This meant that ministers should not turn aside from the books on the Psalms already in use, but rather use Alexander's as a corrective to wrong translation or exposition. He also wanted to preserve more of the Hebrew component and so opted for an amplified translation. This was also intended as a way of reflecting the word order in Hebrew that often determined the emphasis or the overall sense of the sentence. Other discussions, Alexander believed, such as those on the history of interpretation, or a description of the advocates of conflicting viewpoints, could not be comprehended in a volume of the size he was intending to write.

In view of modern discussions on the structure of the Psalter, Alexander expressed some interesting positions regarding its canonical form. He noted that the psalms are all poetry and were to be sung with musical accompaniment. Also, they are all religious songs intended for a permanent place in public worship. The superscriptions, he believed, were integral parts of the composition of the respective psalms. The arrangement of the Psalms was not just fortuitous, as may at first sight appear, and though in some cases it may be hard to find a reason for the juxtaposition of certain psalms, yet often we find double psalms or even trilogies because of similarity of content. His contention was that the psalms were not thrown together in random fashion, even if we cannot discern the principle underlying the structure.

The value of Alexander's *Psalms* lies in his translation as well as in his exegetical comments. He always aimed at what met the needs of ministers and students. The amount of Hebrew is kept to the very minimum, and the meaning of any word is almost invariably given in the context. It differs from his Isaiah commentary in that there is no reference to, or interaction with, other scholarly writing. His intention was to provide a volume with translation and comment that would lead to doctrinal and practical use of the book of Psalms.

Several times in this introduction, Alexander refers to the views of Hengstenberg. His indebtedness to him was great, but he was not afraid to differ from him. Thus, in discussing hypotheses regarding the arrangement of the Psalter, he summarizes Hengstenberg's view, and then says that though it is ingenious, yet it contributes little to the understanding of some of the Psalms.

In the summer of 1857 Addison Alexander went to New York, intending to work on a book on Old Testament history. His journal records what happened.

> *June 1.—Began my book on Old Testament history.*
> *June 2.—Broke down.*
> *June 3.—Resumed my experiment.*
> *June 4.—Broke down again.*

Instead, he wrote on Mark's Gospel, beginning on 16 June and completing it by August. This meant that he was finishing a chapter every four days. He was staying with his brother James in New York, and his nephew, Henry Carrington Alexander, was at home that summer. Henry recalled how his uncle worked in his father's study with his coat off and a jug of iced water beside him. The long table was partially covered with manuscript, 'and his hand was going like a race-horse'. He didn't discuss his work unless answering a specific question from him.

When the commentary on Mark was published in October 1858, his brother James expressed his delight with it in a letter to him:

> *I pronounce this [the commentary on Mark] by far your best work. It is eminently readable. It contains episodical*

> *passages very agreeable to a purist in language. Especially have you hit off the rendering into happy equivalents in sound English. The diction is better than any in your opera [works]. Two qualities are quite unusual: 1. You place the reader (and this is more than any expositor known to me) near the standpunct [German, standpoint, point of view] of a Greek scholar; and 2. You give vividness to the narrative and remove the integument [external covering], or rusty coating, of custom and daily use.*

Addison thought this the highest compliment that had ever been paid to him.

He had another home to go to in New York as his brother Samuel was minister of Fifteenth Street Presbyterian Church. Samuel wrote of how Addison would work at a table near the front window from eight in the morning till five in the afternoon. He seemed oblivious to all the street noise and that of the passing traffic. Having done all his reading during the winter months while lecturing at the seminary, he would only come with his Hebrew Bible and his Greek New Testament. When questioned as to how he could proceed without access to the commentaries he would say, 'I know what they all have said.'

The Lord's Day was kept free from all work. Three times he would attend church services, and the rest of the day would be given over to reading hymns and devotional books. He listened to various preachers, not just the prominent ones, and never spoke critically of any of them. Once he heard a minister preaching on Psalm 1, who made full use of

Addison's comments on it. He said, 'That is what I like; that is what I write my commentaries for.'

Lecturing on Acts was part of Addison's course work on apostolic history. In the preface to the commentary on Acts, he explained his original intent of writing for students and ministers. In changing his plan to make it 'more generally useful', as he wrote, he reduced it in size and omitted matter that would only interest professional or educated readers. This still meant that his commentary was almost 1000 pages in length, and he retained some discussion of the Greek text. His aim in expounding the book was to make comment on the AV translation in order to improve it, 'so as to place the English reader as nearly as possible on the same footing with the student of the Greek text.' While he commented on history and theology, he followed his normal practice of not attempting to include suggestions on the use of particular passages. With his other commentaries he wrote the introduction last, but, as he explained to his publisher Charles Scribner, he had lectured so often on Acts that he could write the introduction at the very outset.

When the *Commentary on the Acts of the Apostles* was reprinted in 1956 (by Zondervan in Grand Rapids), it was highly commended by Dr Theodore Mueller of Concordia Theological Seminary and Dr Henry Schultze of Calvin Theological Seminary. They both thought it belonged amongst the finest commentaries. Much more recently it has been given high praise by the late Dr John Stott. In surveying the literature on Acts, he remarked (in his *The Message of Acts*) that he enjoyed reading some of the older books that were often neglected. He wrote: 'I have appreciated the pithy comments of Johann Albrecht Bengel of the eighteenth century, the godly and clear-headed insights of J. A. Alexander, the brilliant Princeton linguist of the nineteenth century, and the archeological expertise of Sir William Ramsay...' That phrase, 'the godly and clear-headed insights', could be applied not only to Alexander's *Acts*, but also to his Isaiah, Psalms, Mark and Matthew.

In 1857 Addison took up the Gospel of Luke. This was one of the books on which he was to write according to the scheme that had been arranged. On 31 October that year, he recorded in his diary that he had finished his exposition of Luke 2:36-52. However, he changed his mind and started to write on Matthew instead. On 1 December his diary had this entry:

> *Dec. 1 — No lecture. Walked. Read Ezekiel xxv. In Chaldee. Read Giessler, on the* History of the Reformed Churches *and made notes thereon. Laid aside Luke and took up Matthew. Read Erasmus, Calvin, Kuinoel, and Robinson, on parts of Matthew i. Coverdale's Bible, Genesis x. and Matthew i. Hansard, 1828.*

The final reference in that diary entry is interesting, as he was often reading material from earlier periods. Sometimes it was copies of the *Edinburgh Review*, or on others, as on this occasion, debates in the parliament of Westminster.

The comments that follow this entry show something of his amazing activity in the year just drawing to a close. At the seminary he had lectured a hundred and fifty times and examined classes thirty times. He had preached thirty-two times, listened to seventy-five sermons, had written a commentary on the last fifteen chapters of Acts, a commentary on the whole of Mark, and on the first chapter of Matthew. He had been to New York twenty times in addition to spending the whole summer there, to Philadelphia seven times, and to Trenton four times.

After Addison Alexander's death, four volumes of his work appeared posthumously. First, two volumes of sermons, *Sermons, Joseph Addison Alexander, D.D.*, were published in 1860 and reprinted by Solid Ground Christian Books in 2004 with the title, *Theology on Fire: Sermons from the Heart of J. A. Alexander*. A total of forty-three sermons were included, and there is no way of discerning the principle on which the choice was made for inclusion in these volumes. Some of the sermons can be dated because of references in his journal, but many cannot be located in a specific period of his life. It is impossible to know if these sermons are fully representative of his pulpit ministry, though clearly a common style is displayed throughout the ones included.

Second, the commentary on sixteen chapters of Matthew's Gospel that he had completed was published in 1861, including his summary of each of the remaining chapters of the book. On the manuscript, at the commencement of the analysis of Matthew 17, was a note: 'Resumed after five weeks of confinement and inaction, January 3d, 1860'. The manuscript was sent to the publisher by Addison Alexander's brother, Samuel Davis Alexander. It was issued by Charles Scribner in New York and amounted to over 450 pages of very small print. This volume has been reprinted several times.

The style of this incomplete commentary on Matthew was very similar to that in his other commentaries (Mark and Acts), and especially to the volume on Mark. However, it does seem that he used Greek more in this one, though almost always the meaning of the word was given in English. Though the final work on it was done while his health was failing, the quality of the exegesis is no different, nor is there any indication that he was starting to abbreviate his comments. Far from it, as he had an extensive note on Matthew 16:18: 'And I say unto thee, That thou art Peter, and upon this rock I will build my church; and the gates of hell shall not prevail against it.' This note is virtually a mini-essay on the subject extending to about 2500 words. Another feature of this commentary is Alexander's attention to the matter of translation of the Greek text into English. From early on he had a particular interest in the English language and wanted to be able to translate the biblical text in a way that would assist pastors in particular in their understanding of its message. He referred to a variety of translations: Wycliffe, Tyndale, Coverdale, Cranmer, the Bishops' Bible, Geneva and Rheims. For example, in dealing with Matthew 16:3: 'And in the morning, (It will be) foul weather today: for the sky is red and lowering,' he noted: 'The older versions have a rich variety of English phrases to express this appearance of the heavens. Wiclif, *heaven shineth heavily*; Tyndale, *the sky is cloudy and red*; Geneva, *red and cloudy*; Cranmer, *glowing red*; Rheims, *the element doth glow and lower.*' Among his last readings was Coverdale's version of the Old Testament.

Third, notes of some of his lectures on the New Testament and church history were edited after his death by his brother Samuel and published in 1867. This volume has been digitized, and it can be reprinted on demand. While there are interesting parts in *Notes on New Testament Literature and Ecclesiastical History*, yet it was a mistake to make them available in book form. The reason for this is that Addison Alexander himself had not got them to a stage where he was ready to publish. He was under pressure to complete the commentaries he had agreed to write, and as he was continuing to amass more information on these subjects, he was not ready to commit them to a completed publishable manuscript. Also, the form of the notes, which includes questions, showed that it was intended for classroom discussion, not a wider readership. One important thing these notes do show, however, is that he was reading the latest scholarly discussions from the United States, Britain and the Continent right up to the end.

Charles Hodge, writing after Addison's death, observed that he was cut off in a very productive time of life, and that a lot could have been expected from him in the next ten years had he lived. If he had finished his commentary on Matthew, it may well have been back to Luke's Gospel that he turned again, having at least made a start on a commentary on it. Then he needed to write on John's Gospel if he was to complete his part of the plan he had devised with Charles Hodge and his brother James to write jointly on the whole of the New Testament.

9.
His preaching

It is hard to judge preaching in previous times because of the limitations that are forced upon us. We do not have recordings of sermons, and so must depend on eyewitness accounts, records of the effect of sermons, or printed addresses. Also, we need to assess the sermons of past preachers against the standards and conventions of their own day, not by what we know of preaching in our day.

For Addison Alexander we do have various reports from his hearers of the quality of his preaching, and two volumes of his sermons were printed. But another difficulty arises concerning those two volumes, for we cannot be sure that he delivered the sermons exactly as they are printed. He had a phenomenal memory, and at times he may have preached without notes but yet followed very closely the written sermon he had prepared. On one particular occasion no one turned up to preach in the First Church, Princeton, on a Sunday evening. After some delay, one of the elders approached Dr Alexander to see if he would preach, but he declined. Various others also declined, and then Addison Alexander was again approached and went into the pulpit and preached, as an eyewitness later wrote, 'with an earnestness, an unction, and a power that I never heard him surpass.' This was probably not a case of extemporaneous preaching but an exhibition of his wonderful memory being put to use as he recalled one of his own sermons.

After Addison's death an acquaintance, Dr John Leyburn, referred to his style of preaching. Leyburn drew attention to the crowds who came to hear him when he preached for a year in Philadelphia (1836), when the churches and even the vestibules were filled. This is his description of Addison's style:

> *In his manner there was nothing of what are considered the graces of oratory. He usually read his sermons closely, without action, and in a rapid monotonous tone; but the copiousness of thought, the affluence of the language, and the richness and vividness of his imagination, charmed every one. It was as if one were listening to a Macaulay, discoursing from the pulpit on the sublimest of themes.*

A later hearer was Dr Robert Dabney, who listened to two of his sermons while Addison Alexander was on a visit to Virginia in 1855. The two men spent parts of two days together, and Dabney, while acknowledging that Addison was 'a truly unobtrusive and retiring man,' yet found him a very pleasant conversationalist. His comment on the sermons was this:

> *I found his sermons characterized by very thorough and evidently faithful preparation, scholarly finish of style, and fine, discriminating acumen in the criticism and exposition of scriptural propositions. I may say, once for all, that these have always struck me as the prominent traits of his critical writings, with (also) laborious, painstaking diligence, and profound reverence for the very words of Scripture.*

The printed sermons are all approximately twenty printed pages in length, and on average take about forty minutes to read out loud. The language at many points would baffle modern congregations as it was so scholarly. Here is an example, the opening paragraph of a sermon on 1 John 3:2: 'It doth not yet appear what we shall be.'

> *These words admit of being taken either in a wide and comprehensive, or a more restricted and specific sense, as referring to a blessed immortality beyond the grave, or to futurity in general, including the as yet unknown vicissitudes belonging to the present state of our existence. It is in this large application of the language, and indeed with special reference to a proximate futurity, that I invite your attention to the fact that 'it doth not yet appear what we shall be'.*

The printed sermons reveal several characteristics. Alexander always started with the text of Scripture, and normally at the end of the sermon came back to it. Most sermons were not divided up into sections, though in some there are enumerated points in a particular section of a sermon. For example, when preaching on Luke 9:60: 'Let the dead bury their dead, but go thou and preach the kingdom of God', he made several points concerning the teaching of the text:

1. That there is still a special call of Christ to individuals, not only to believe in him, but to preach his kingdom;
2. This vocation, where it really exists, is paramount to every personal and selfish plan, to every natural affection, even the most tender, which conflicts with it;
3. That this conflict is not usually unavoidable, though often so regarded by fanatics. The first duty of the Christian is not to desire or create, but to avoid it; but if unavoidable, his next is to obey God rather than man;
4. Our Saviour did not deal indiscriminately with all cases of desire to enter his immediate service. The remark is at least as old as Calvin, that in this case he repelled the man who wanted to go with him everywhere, and urged the man to follow him at once, who wanted to go home for what appeared to be most necessary purposes. So far as his example is a guide to us in these things, we are bound not only to persuade, but to discourage as the case may be;
5. There is no more danger of excluding those whom God has called by faithful presentation of the whole truth, than there is of preventing conversion of his chosen ones, by showing them the true tests of faith and repentance.

At times he could take a biblical passage and apply the teaching in a very striking way. A case in point is the question asked by the wise men when they came to Jerusalem: 'Where is he that is born king of the Jews?' (Matt. 2:2). When the question was originally asked, the answer would have been 'in Bethlehem of Judah, in a stable, in a manger'. But when asked at the crucifixion, the response would have been — 'there, there, upon that cross.' When the eleven disciples were left alone on the Mount of Olives after the ascension, if they had been asked the question, they would have pointed upwards, and replied: 'He is in heaven.' He ended the sermon by asking whether anything could stem the advance of the kingdom of the Lord Jesus, and his response was:

> *No, let Bethlehem, and Calvary, and Olivet, and Paradise, and Christendom, and Jewry all bear witness, that what he was born to bring about must come to pass; the day, though distant, shall arrive when the kingdoms of the world are to become the kingdoms of our Lord, and of his Christ; and when the joint Hallelujah of angels and men, of the church on earth, and of the church in heaven, of Jews and Gentiles, shall proclaim the final and eternal answer to the question, Where is he that is born king of the Jews?*

The printed sermons do not contain any illustrations. This is not conclusive evidence that he did not use them, as his father, Archibald Alexander, definitely did so, though they are not included in his published sermons. With a mind as vigorous as his, it would be strange if he excluded all illustrative material from his spoken addresses.

He often preached for his brothers, James and Samuel, in New York, who enjoyed listening to him. On one occasion in December 1853 James commented: 'Addison preached a grand sermon for me yesterday. He is very unequal.' That comment is interesting, because James felt that his brother was becoming overly exegetical in his preaching, at least as far as popular audiences were concerned. He commented that Addison himself was not happy to fall back upon 'the more florid and animated discourses of the kind he used to preach in Philadelphia, and was consequently getting to think that his forte was the lecture-room and not the pulpit.' This confirms the feeling that, at times, he was far more vigorous and animated in the pulpit than at other times, and his brother James was well aware of this. Again, this seems to confirm the strong impression that educated audiences may well have listened avidly to his 'florid' discourses, whereas country parishioners were looking for something more practical and down-to-earth. Just as Benjamin Franklin, though not a Christian believer, was attracted by the preaching of George Whitefield in the previous century, so there were many in Princeton, Philadelphia and New York who found pleasure in listening to Addison Alexander's beautifully worded sermons.

At times he pressed home the gospel offer to his hearers. Once, when preaching in the college chapel in Princeton, he urged them to respond to the invitation to the feast. In speaking on Luke 14:17, 'Come for all things are now ready,' he spoke of the readiness of all things as a reason for coming, and yet the sinner's reluctance to come. He then addressed this appeal to the congregation:

> *But to you who own yourself a sinner, and in need of mercy, and expect to find it one day in the Saviour, to you I put the question — and would pray that you would put it to yourselves: — what prevents your coming now? What invisible hand drags you back when you are almost on the threshold? — holds your eyes fast shut when you begin to see light; stifles your very cries for mercy; and chokes down the throbbings of your bursting heart; — and what is it?*

> *No external force; you act freely in refusing to come. What inward cause, then — why do you not come? What keeps you still away?*

Whereas his father was more at home in country congregations, Addison was certainly more at ease in the town and city churches. Philadelphia was the largest city in the United States in his lifetime, and it was also regarded as the cultural capital. He often preached there, and the type of sermons he preached is probably well represented in the two volumes that appeared after his death, *Theology on Fire*. These volumes show a style more like R. S. Candlish or Thomas Guthrie in Scotland in the same era, than the simplicity of Robert Murray M'Cheyne or of J. C. Ryle. There appears to have been some tension in his mind over his sermon preparation, for the man who could entertain children with his stories seemed to find it difficult to drop down to the level of ordinary adults.

Addison Alexander did not enter into debate about current political issues or government decisions from the pulpit. On one occasion, however, he did comment on the idea that was becoming prevalent in the middle of the nineteenth century that America was almost to be identified with God's chosen people. Opposing the idea that America was virtually to be equated with Israel, he said,

> *Such is the force of words, to influence as well as to express thought, that by dint of constant repetition, men may actually come at last to think themselves a chosen and peculiar people, not only in the spiritual Christian sense, but in the national external sense.*

10.
Assessment of his life

In the books he wrote and bequeathed to future generations is the legacy of a brilliant scholar. There can be very few who at such an early age have worked with so many languages, have read and written on so many varied topics, and have taught such a range of biblical and theological topics. During his years as a faculty member of Princeton Theological Seminary he was in turn the professor of Old Testament, Church History and New Testament. He was a genius who seemed to find assimilation of knowledge and retention of it so easy. As Charles Hodge said of him, if he wanted to, he could grasp and teach any subject.

Some have referred to him as an eccentric genius. This is largely because of two factors. The first was his propensity for change — change of dwelling, change of his library, change in course work. This demonstrated itself right through his life, and it must at times have been a distraction from his main work. The second factor was his social relationships. It is true that at times he was somewhat of a recluse. He often did not eat with the rest of his family.

But 'eccentric' seems too strong a word and with connotations that do not apply to Addison Alexander. To be an 'eccentric' is to be off-centre, whereas he was extremely focussed on the main issues of life. From the time of his conversion in 1830 he was committed to Christ and subject to God's Word. While in some things he was changeable, in other things he was not. He was a stickler for time, starting and finishing lectures on the hour. When he was back in his old home after his father's death, when the bell was rung for family worship he came out of his study immediately and assumed the role of leading it by reading from Scripture and leading in prayer.

The contrast in Addison Alexander's life between the very disciplined scholar and the wandering tourist is strange. He could only achieve his devotion to study and writing by exercising strict control of his time each day, and his diary is testimony to the amount of study and reading he achieved, day after day, year after year. In some inexplicable way his desire for novelty, and especially his tours in the summer vacation period, served as a counterfoil to his regimen of intense academic activity.

Three assessments of him by his mentor, Charles Hodge, are worthy of quotation, two coming just after his death and the other some years later. This is the first comment.

> *In all my intercourse with men, though it has been limited, both in this country and Europe, I never met with one having such a combination of wonderful gifts. The grace of God most to be admired was that, though of necessity perfectly familiar with all the forms of error held by the enemies of*

> *truth, and especially the most insidious one of criticism, he had a most simple, child-like faith in the Scriptures, and the deepest reverence for the Word of God. Above all, his crowning glory was his spirituality and devoted piety. We cannot properly estimate our loss till we think of what he was, and what he would have been, for he was only fifty-two years old, and the next ten years is the best period of such a man's life.*

The second comment came in a letter to Dr Robert L. Dabney of Union Seminary. Hodge and his colleagues, in assessing the needs of the Princeton Seminary, had come to the position that Dabney should be invited to join the faculty. In writing to him on 24 March 1860, Hodge began his letter with these words:

> *You can well understand what an overwhelming blow the unexpected death of Dr Addison Alexander was to all connected with this Seminary. He was our dependence, our delight and our glory. And I doubt not you have deeply sympathized with us in our affliction.*

At the end of this same letter, Hodge makes some very interesting observations on Addison Alexander. He was pleading with Dabney to come to the aid of Princeton Seminary, especially so that he would blend the teaching of both history and theology. This is what he wrote:

> *There is one consideration which weighs with great force on my mind. You are not only a historian, but a theologian. Dr Alexander, of set purpose, would not turn his mind to philosophical or theological subjects. In him, with his*

> *wonderful gifts and attainments, and with the firm faith which he had by early training and by his religious experience, in our system of doctrine, this was of the less account. He, however, never wrote on any theological subject, never exerted himself in the explication or defence of our peculiar faith (except, of course, in his expositions and lectures), or in the refutation of opposing views. This dissociation of theological and historical learning is, of course, in itself, very undesirable, and their union in your case is one of the many reasons which satisfy my judgment that you are eminently qualified to fill the post to which we are so anxious you may come.*

A few years later in a sermon, Hodge again commented on Alexander's life. He said,

> *I believe I was rash enough to say on the floor of the General Assembly of 1860, that I thought Dr Addison Alexander the greatest man whom I had ever seen. This was unwise: both because there are so many different kinds of greatness: and because I was no competent judge. I feel to say now, however, that I never saw a man who so constantly impressed me with a sense of his mental superiority—with his power to acquire knowledge and his power to communicate it. He seemed able to learn anything and to teach anything he pleased.*

The accusation that he was a recluse has also to be challenged. While he may not have sought out company, yet time and again people testified that they had been in his company when he was most companionable and took part in lively conversation. It is true that early on at least, his students were frightened of their brilliant professor, and may well have considered him cold and unapproachable. However, later in his teaching career students were following him out from lectures and engaging in conversation with him.

He certainly had a sense of humour. His nephew, Henry Carrington Alexander, told how he could hear him often laughing away in his study at what he was reading. Some of his writing also displays humour. He told his brother James about preaching in Philadelphia on a hot summer's day. He was being taken to the church by an elder who explained that because it was Sunday, he didn't hire a carriage, and so they had to walk. Addison said that he would make sure that the next time he was to preach it would be on a Wednesday!

Another aspect of his character needs emphasis and that was his relationship with children. As a bachelor he had tremendous rapport with children, and went to great lengths in telling them stories, hand-writing 'journals' for them, and singing to them in a variety of languages. No mention is ever made of him frightening, in any way, the children whom he met.

Addison Alexander was deeply attached to his own family. He had a very close relationship with his brother James, and especially after his father's death, he took particular care of his mother. His reserve with adults contrasts sharply with his openness with children. There is no hint of any romantic relationship, and he never married.

When he died he was only fifty-one years of age. The main legacy he left was four major biblical commentaries (Isaiah, Psalms, Acts and Mark) and an unfinished one on

Matthew. He served as an exemplar to those who followed him, especially to those in the Old Testament departments of Princeton and Westminster Theological Seminaries. The names of William Henry Green, Robert Dick Wilson, Oswald Allis and Edward Young draw attention to succeeding scholars who were undoubtedly influenced by him. They demonstrated the same commitment to God's Word, and also the same dedication to acquiring the necessary linguistic and philological knowledge for the defence and propagation of the faith.

It is almost impossible to know when Addison Alexander's ill-health started to display itself. He certainly did not take good care of himself, and though there are references in his diary to him going for a walk, yet lack of exercise may well have been a negative factor. He doesn't seem to have followed the example of his own father, who until the later years of his life walked each morning and went riding on his horse. Books and study dominated Addison Alexander's life. In the last few years before his death and when his health was failing, he still endeavoured to keep up the same regimen of study that he had from boyhood days. Even his self-imposed programme of commentary writing was continued till the end, up to seven or eight days before his death.

While aware of events within and without the Presbyterian Church, and attending and taking part in local presbytery meetings, he never sought nomination as a commissioner to the General Assembly of the Presbyterian Church. That role he left to others from Princeton Seminary, like his father and Charles Hodge. This was not a sphere in which he was comfortable, for he knew his own limitations.

Aspects of his character were unusual, yet we can look back to a life devoted to biblical scholarship and preparation of students for Christian ministry. Probably his greatest influence was on those who were academic achievers, including those who afterwards became faculty members in colleges or seminaries, or who served in overseas missions. Together with his mentor, Charles Hodge, he was able to speak of Continental theologians and biblical scholars and to utilize their work in the interests of evangelical scholarship. The aim of his biblical commentaries was to help ministers in particular to have fresh understanding of Scripture. These were tools he provided for their teaching and preaching.

A final comment needs to be made. The life and influence of Joseph Addison Alexander cannot be understood merely by looking at his unique contribution. He was one of a very gifted team of scholars who formed the faculty of Princeton Theological Seminary in its first fifty years. For a time he, his father Archibald and his brother James served together (1849–51). Samuel Miller, Charles Hodge, John Breckenridge, A. T. McGill and William Henry Green added their skills and abilities to those of the Alexander family, and so contributed to the influence of the seminary. Addison Alexander was part of a team, and his life, work and influence can only be assessed within that context.

List of available writings of J. A. Alexander

A Commentary on the Acts of the Apostles (Edinburgh: Banner of Truth Trust, 1984).

Essays on the Primitive Church Offices (Scholarly Publishing Office, University of Michigan Library, 2006).

A Geography of the Bible: Compiled for the American Sunday School Union, with his brother James as co-author (Philadelphia: ASSU, 1830; reprinted Delhi: Pranava Books, n.d.).

Isaiah (Grand Rapids: Kregel Publications, 1994).

Mark (Edinburgh: Banner of Truth, 1984).

Matthew (James Family Christian Publishers: 1979).

Notes on New Testament Literature and Ecclesiastical History (Memphis: General Books, 2010).

The Psalms (Scholarly Publishing Office, University of Michigan Library, 2006).

Theology on Fire: Sermons from the Heart of J. A. Alexander, 2 vols. (Birmingham, AL; Solid Ground Christian Books, 2004).

Select bibliography

Henry Carrington Alexander, *The Life of Joseph Addison Alexander*, 2 vols (New York: Charles Scribner, 1870).

David B. Calhoun, *Princeton Seminary: Volume 1 Faith and Learning 1812–1868* (Edinburgh: Banner of Truth Trust, 1994).

John Hall, ed., *Forty years' familiar letters of James W. Alexander, D.D., constituting with notes, a memoir of his life*, 2 vols (Scholarly Publishing Office, University of Michigan Library, 2006).

J. H. Moorehead, 'Joseph Addison Alexander: Common Sense, Romanticism and Biblical Criticism at Princeton', *Journal of Presbyterian History 53* (1975), pp. 51-65.

Marian Taylor, *The Old Testament in the Old Princeton School* (1812-1929), (San Francisco: Mellen Research

University Press, 1992), especially 'Chapter 3 — Joseph Addison Alexander', pp. 89-166.

E. J. Young, 'The Study of Isaiah since the time of Joseph Addison Alexander', *Westminster Theological Journal* 9 (1946), pp. 1-9.